I0017433

Apress Pocket Guides

Apress Pocket Guides present concise summaries of cutting-edge developments and working practices throughout the tech industry. Shorter in length, books in this series aims to deliver quick-to-read guides that are easy to absorb, perfect for the time-poor professional.

This series covers the full spectrum of topics relevant to the modern industry, from security, AI, machine learning, cloud computing, web development, product design, to programming techniques and business topics too.

Typical topics might include:

- A concise guide to a particular topic, method, function or framework

- Professional best practices and industry trends

- A snapshot of a hot or emerging topic

- Industry case studies

- Concise presentations of core concepts suited for students and those interested in entering the tech industry

- Short reference guides outlining 'need-to-know' concepts and practices.

More information about this series at https://link.springer.com/bookseries/17385.

Creational Design Patterns in C#

Building Flexible and Scalable Software

Vaskaran Sarcar

Apress®

Creational Design Patterns in C#: Building Flexible and Scalable Software

Vaskaran Sarcar
Kolkata, West Bengal, India

ISBN-13 (pbk): 979-8-8688-1566-9   ISBN-13 (electronic): 979-8-8688-1567-6
https://doi.org/10.1007/979-8-8688-1567-6

Managing Director, Apress Media LLC: Welmoed Spahr
Acquisitions Editor: Smriti Srivastava
Coordinating Editor: Jessica Vakili

Cover designed by eStudioCalamar

Distributed to the book trade worldwide by Springer Science+Business Media New York, 1 New York Plaza, New York, NY 10004. Phone 1-800-SPRINGER, fax (201) 348-4505, e-mail orders-ny@springer-sbm.com, or visit www.springeronline.com. Apress Media, LLC is a Delaware LLC and the sole member (owner) is Springer Science + Business Media Finance Inc (SSBM Finance Inc). SSBM Finance Inc is a **Delaware** corporation.

For information on translations, please e-mail booktranslations@springernature.com; for reprint, paperback, or audio rights, please e-mail bookpermissions@springernature.com.

Apress titles may be purchased in bulk for academic, corporate, or promotional use. eBook versions and licenses are also available for most titles. For more information, reference our Print and eBook Bulk Sales web page at http://www.apress.com/bulk-sales.

Any source code or other supplementary material referenced by the author in this book is available to readers on GitHub (https://github.com/Apress). For more detailed information, please visit https://www.apress.com/gp/services/source-code.

To my wife Indrani, who sometimes disturbs my mental peace and embarrasses me. However, she takes care of me and welcomes a simple life to help me grow as an author.

Table of Contents

About the Author

 **Vaskaran Sarcar** obtained his master's in engineering from Jadavpur University, Kolkata (India), and his master's in computer application from Vidyasagar University, Midnapore (India). He was a National Gate Scholar (2007–2009) and has over 12 years of experience in education and the IT industry. He devoted his early years (2005–2007) to the teaching profession at various engineering colleges, and later, he joined HP India PPS R&D Hub in Bangalore. He worked there for more than 10 years and became a senior software engineer and team lead. After that, he pursued his passion. Vaskaran has already authored 16 Apress books that can be found at amazon.com/author/vaskaran_sarcar or https://link.springer.com/search?newsearch=true&query=vaskaran+sarcar&content-type=book&dateFrom=&dateTo=&sortBy=newestFirst. You can also find him on LinkedIn at https://www.linkedin.com/in/vaskaransarcar.

About the Technical Reviewer

Shekhar Kumar Maravi is a Software Architect focused on design and development, whose main interests are programming languages, Linux system programming, Linux kernel, algorithms, and data structures. He obtained his master's degree in Computer Science and Engineering from Indian Institute of Technology Bombay. After graduation, he joined Hewlett-Packard's R&D Hub in India to work on Printer Firmware. Currently, he is a Product & Solution Development Team Lead for automated pathology lab diagnostic devices at Siemens Healthcare R&D division. He can be reached via LinkedIn at https://www.linkedin.com/in/shekharmaravi.

Acknowledgments

First, I thank the Almighty. I believe that I was able to complete this book with His blessings. I extend my deepest gratitude and thanks to the following people:

Shekhar – He is the technical reviewer for this book and reviewed many of my other books. Whenever I was in need, he provided support. He answered all my queries over the phone, on WhatsApp, and in emails. Thank you one more time.

Smriti, Jessica, Celestin, and the Apress team – I sincerely thank each of you for giving me another opportunity to work with you.

Nirmal, Jagathesan, MohanKumar and the copy editor Ann Gemer – Thanks to each of you for your exceptional support in beautifying my work. Your efforts are extraordinary.

Finally, I thank the people from various online communities, particularly the C# developer community, the .NET developer community, and the Stack Overflow community, who share their knowledge in different forms. In fact, I thank everyone who directly or indirectly contributed to this work.

Introduction

Welcome to your journey through *Creational Design Patterns in C#*. You probably know that the concept of design patterns became popular with the Gang of Four's famous book *Design Patterns: Elements of Reusable Object-Oriented Software* (Addison-Wesley, 1994). The book was published at the end of 1994, and it primarily focused on C++. Many of these patterns are the basis of today's programming world. So, it's unsurprising that it stays on Amazon's bestseller list.

On the other hand, C# had its first major release (C# 2.0) in 2005. Since then, it has become rich with new features and is now a popular programming language. I also wrote several books on design patterns using C# and Java. Then why did I write this book?

First, those books covered all the Gang of Four (GoF) patterns, along with some additional patterns. The inclusion of so many patterns made those books fat (yes, they are over 600 pages). However, we are living in a busy world, and there are plenty of distractions. Holding the focus for a prolonged time by overcoming those distractions is becoming challenging day by day. So, it is no wonder that many people are afraid of fat books. Next, nowadays, programming languages have lots of new features. You may think: Do I still need all these patterns? The answer is no. In fact, many of these patterns were marked as peripheral. Last but not least, over the years, I have received a lot of constructive feedback from my readers.

Keeping these points in mind, I decided to write pocketbooks on some selected design patterns. The book you are reading now is the result of that decision.

The classical GoF book cataloged 23 patterns into three categories – Creational, Structural, and Behavioral. They grouped five patterns under the creational patterns: Abstract Factory, Factory Method, Prototype, Builder, and Singleton. The creational patterns are about the creation of objects (yes, though the Singleton pattern restricts the number of objects, it is still creational). At a high level, these patterns abstract the instantiation process and help you make the systems independent from how their objects are composed, created, and represented. To illustrate, while implementing these patterns, you normally ask: "Where should I place the **'new'** keyword in my application?" This decision can determine the degree of coupling of your classes.

Over the period, the Abstract Factory was considered a peripheral design pattern (see Design Patterns 15 Years Later: An Interview with Erich Gamma, Richard Helm, and Ralph Johnson I InformIT). So, I did not discuss this pattern in this pocketbook. Instead, I included another useful pattern, called Dependency Injection. It is interesting to note that later, one of the GoF authors, Ralph Johnson, acknowledged that the name of this pattern (DI) came out after their book was published. He also stated that they'd like to include DI in the second edition of their book (see JDD2015 - Twenty-one Years of Design Patterns (Ralph Johnson) - YouTube). This is why **this book covers four GoF patterns and one non-GoF pattern**.

How Is the Book Organized?

To give you an idea about the contents of this book, let me summarize the following points:

Chapter 1 explains the need for a factory. It demystifies the simple factory idiom (which is not actually a pattern) and ends with a Factory Method implementation.

Chapter 2 discusses the Singleton pattern with four different implementations.

Chapter 3 illustrates two different implementations of the Builder pattern.

Chapter 4 shows you a Prototype pattern implementation and points out the differences between a shallow copy and a deep copy. This chapter also compares the Prototype and Factory Method patterns.

Chapter 5 explains the Dependency Injection pattern with five different implementations and compares the techniques.

You can enjoy learning when you analyze the implementations and ask questions (about the doubts). So, throughout this book, you will see many "Q&A Sessions." Each question in these Q&A sessions is marked with **Q<chapter_no>.<Question_no>**. For example, **Q3.2** means question number 2 of Chapter 3. These are presented to make your future learning easier and enjoyable, but most importantly, they make you confident as a developer.

You can download all the book's source code from the publisher's website: `https://github.com/Apress/Creational-Design-Patterns-in-C-Sharp`.

Prerequisite Knowledge

I expect you to be familiar with C# and how to compile or run a C# application in Visual Studio. This book does not invest time in easily available topics, such as how to install Visual Studio on your system or how to write a "Hello World" program. In short, the target readers of this book are those who have an idea about the pure object-oriented concepts like polymorphism, inheritance, abstraction, and encapsulation. I want you to make the most out of C# by harnessing the power of both object-oriented programming (OOP) and functional programming (FP).

Who This Book Is For

You can read this book if the answer is yes to the following questions:

- Are you familiar with .NET, C#, and basic object-oriented concepts like polymorphism, inheritance, abstraction, and encapsulation?

- Do you know how to set up your coding environment?

- Are you interested in knowing how the modern-day constructs of C# can help you implement useful creational patterns?

You probably shouldn't read this book if the answer is yes to any of the following questions:

- Are you looking for a C# tutorial or reference book?

- Are you looking for a book that covers all GoF patterns or the patterns that were not mentioned earlier?

- "I do not like Windows, Visual Studio, and/or .NET. I want to explore design patterns without them." Is this statement true for you?

Guidelines for Using This Book

Here are some suggestions so that you can get the most out of this book:

- Sequential reading of these chapters can help you learn faster. This is because some useful and related topics may have already been discussed in a previous chapter, and I have not repeated those discussions in the later chapters.

- The programs in this book should give you the expected output in the upcoming versions of C#/Visual Studio as well. Though I believe that these results should not vary in other environments, you know the nature of software: it is naughty! So, I recommend that if you want to see the same output, it will be better if you can mimic the same environment.

Useful Software

These are the important software/tools that I used for this book:

- All the programs were tested with C# 13 and .NET 9. During the development of this book, software updates kept coming, and I also kept updating. When I finished my draft, I had the latest edition of Microsoft Visual Studio Community 2022 (64-bit) (Version 17.13.5).

- The good news for you is that this community edition is free of cost. If you do not use the Windows operating system, you can also use Visual Studio Code, a source code editor developed by Microsoft that runs on Windows, macOS, and Linux operating systems. This multi-platform IDE is also free. However, I recommend that you check the license and privacy statement as well. This is because this statement may change in the future.

- You can download and install the Visual Studio IDE from Download Visual Studio Tools - Install Free for Windows, Mac, Linux. You are expected to get Figure 1.

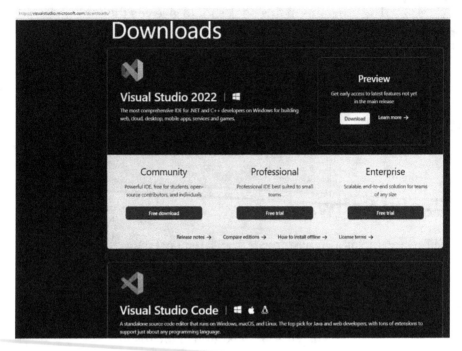

Figure 1. *The official download link for Visual Studio 2022 and Visual Studio Code*

Note   At the time of this writing, this link works fine, and the information is correct. However, the link and policies may change in the future. The same comment applies to all the mentioned links in this book.

I used Visual Studio's Class Designer tool to generate class diagrams in this book. You can learn about it from Design, visualize, & refactor with Class Designer - Visual Studio (Windows) | Microsoft Learn.

Conventions Used in This Book

Here, I mention only a few points: In some places, to avoid more typing, I have used only the pronoun "he" to refer to a person when the context is generic, for example, a customer, an executive, etc.

Secondly, in many places, I have given you Microsoft's documentation links. Why? For me, as the creator, these are the authenticated sources of information to describe a feature.

Finally, all the programs, corresponding outputs, and important notes of the book follow the same font and structure. To draw your attention, in some places, I have made them bold. For example, consider the following code fragment (taken from Chapter 5 where I will discuss the constructor injection technique):

```
using static System.Console;
class Driver(IVehicle vehicle)
{
    private readonly IVehicle _vehicle = vehicle;
    public void Drive(int speed)
    {
        WriteLine($"The driver can drive a {_vehicle.
        Run(speed)}");
    }
}
```

Final Words

You are an intelligent person. You have chosen a topic that can assist you throughout your career. As you learn and review these concepts, I suggest you write your code; only then will you master this area. There is no shortcut for this. Do you know the ancient story of Euclid and Ptolemy, ruler of Egypt? Euclid's approach to mathematics was based on logical reasoning and rigorous proofs, and Ptolemy asked Euclid if there was an easier way to learn mathematics. Euclid's reply to the ruler? **"There is no royal road to geometry."** Though you are not studying geometry, the essence of this reply applies here. You must study these concepts and code. Do not give up when you face challenges. They are the indicators that you are growing better.

Errata: I have tried my level best to ensure the accuracy of the content. However, mistakes can happen. So, I have a plan to maintain the "Errata," and if required, I can also make some updates/announcements there. So, I suggest that you visit those pages to receive any important corrections or updates.

An Appeal: You can easily understand that any good quality work takes many days and many months (even years!). Many authors like me invest most of their time in writing and heavily depend on it. You can encourage and help these authors by preventing piracy. If you come across any illegal copies of our works in any form on the Internet, I would be grateful if you would provide me/the Apress team with the location address or website name. In this context, you can use the link `https://www.apress.com/gp/services/rights-permission/piracy` as well.

Share Your Feedback: The book is designed so that upon its completion, you will develop an adequate knowledge of creational design patterns using C# and .NET. I hope that you will value the effort. Once you finish reading this book, I request that you provide valuable feedback on the Amazon review page or any other platform you like.

CHAPTER 1

Factory Method Pattern

The Factory Method pattern is one of the most useful patterns for developers. This chapter discusses this pattern using simple examples.

Concept

The importance of this pattern will become clear once you understand the following:

- Why do you need a factory?

- How can you use the Simple Factory pattern?

This is why this chapter answers these questions before showing you an implementation of the Factory Method pattern.

Programming Without a Factory

Consider a company that makes different types of vehicles, such as cars and motorcycles. Let's start the discussion using a program that does not use a factory. You're probably most familiar with it because you directly use the new operator each time you instantiate an object.

© Vaskaran Sarcar 2025
V. Sarcar, *Creational Design Patterns in C#*, Apress Pocket Guides,
https://doi.org/10.1007/979-8-8688-1567-6_1

The Common Code

In this chapter, you'll see three different demonstrations. To reuse the code, I created a class library project called VehicleLibrary. This library has an abstract class, called Vehicle, that is as follows:

```
namespace VehicleLibrary
{
    public abstract class Vehicle
    {
        protected string type = "Not defined";
        public abstract void Display();
    }
}
```

Two classes – Car and Motorcycle – inherit from this interface. First, see the Car class:

```
using static System.Console;

namespace VehicleLibrary
{
    public class Car : Vehicle
    {
        public Car()
        {
            type = "car";
        }
        public override void Display()
        {
            WriteLine($"A {this} is created.");
        }
        public override string ToString()
        {
```

```
            return type;
        }
    }
}
```

The Motorcycle class maintains a similar structure:

```
using static System.Console;

namespace VehicleLibrary
{
    public class Motorcycle : Vehicle
    {
        public Motorcycle()
        {
            type = "motorcycle";
        }

        public override void Display()
        {
            WriteLine($"A {this} is created.");
        }

        public override string ToString()
        {
            return type;
        }
    }
}
```

To make things easy, let's see the class diagram (Figure 1-1) as well.

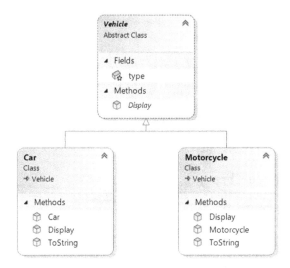

Figure 1-1. *The Car and Motorcycle classes inherit from the IVehicle interface*

POINT TO NOTE

In Demonstration 1, you'll see me using the VehicleLibrary. In the SimpleFactoryLibrary of Demonstration 2 and in the FactoryMethodLibrary of Demonstration 3, I'll also use the Vehicle class of this library. This is why I showed the common code before you see any demonstration in this chapter. I remind you that I have used Visual Studio's class designer tool to generate class diagrams in this book.

Demonstration 1

Now see a program (FP_Demo1_Client.cs) that uses the VehicleLibrary as follows:

// FP_Demo1_Client.cs

```
using VehicleLibrary;
using static System.Console;
```

```
WriteLine("Understanding the need of factories.\n");

Vehicle? vehicle = CreateAndDisplayVehicle("car");
WriteLine($"The {vehicle} construction process is completed.");

WriteLine("-----------");

vehicle = CreateAndDisplayVehicle("motorcycle");
WriteLine($"The {vehicle} construction process is completed.");

static Vehicle? CreateAndDisplayVehicle(string type)
{
    Vehicle? vehicle = null;
    if (type == "car")
    {
        vehicle = new Car();
    }
    if (type == "motorcycle")
    {
        vehicle = new Motorcycle();
    }
    vehicle?.Display();
    return vehicle;
}
```

POINT TO NOTE

This book heavily uses top-level statements. Using this syntax, you can place the executable code at the top of your file, i.e., from line number 1. Hence, these are "top-level" statements. As a result, you can reduce code by removing the Main class. If you are new to it, I suggest you learn more about it from the online link Top-level statements tutorial - C# | Microsoft Learn.

Output

There is no surprise that when you execute this program, you'll see the following output:

```
Understanding the need of factories.

A car is created.
The car construction process is completed.
-----------
A motorcycle is created.
The motorcycle construction process is completed.
```

Analysis

Let me ask you a few questions. **If you need a different type of vehicle (e.g., a bus), how can you proceed?** Probably, you'll introduce a new if block such as

```
if (type == "bus")
{
    vehicle = new Bus();
}
```

OK. Let me ask you another question: **If the company decides to stop the production of cars (or motorcycles), how can you proceed?** Probably, you'll delete the corresponding if block.

Now you understand that you may need to make changes inside the CreateAndDisplayVehicle method very often. Let me highlight the region of our concern in bold:

```
static Vehicle? CreateAndDisplayVehicle(string type)
{
    Vehicle? vehicle = null;
    if (type == "car")
```

```
{
    vehicle = new Car();
}
if (type == "motorcycle")
{
    vehicle = new Motorcycle();
}
vehicle?.Display();
return vehicle;
}
```

Let's see how you can tackle this in the upcoming demonstration.

Q&A Session

Q1.1 To compare the values of strings, you used the equality operator (==) instead of the String.Equals method. Is there any reason behind this?

In C#, if you want to compare the values of the string objects, you can use the equality operator == instead of String.Equals. The official link Built-in reference types - C# reference | Microsoft Learn confirms this by saying the following:

> *Although string is a reference type, the* equality operators == and != *are defined to compare the values of string objects, not references. Value based equality makes testing for string equality more intuitive.*

Simple Factory Implementation

This is the time to introduce the Simple Factory pattern. Before that, let me help you understand the concept of a factory.

What Is a Factory?

In object-oriented programming (OOP), a factory is an object that can create other objects. A factory can be invoked in many ways, but it often uses a method that can return objects with varying prototypes. Any subroutine that can help us create these new objects can be considered a factory. Most importantly, it abstracts the process of object creation from the application's consumers. Let me give you some examples.

Real-Life Example

In a South Indian restaurant, when you order your favorite biryani dish, the waiter may ask whether you like your biryani with more spice or less spice. Based on your choice, the chef will add spices to the core material and make the appropriate dish for you.

Let's consider another example: when a kid demands a toy from his parent, the kid does not know how the parent will fulfill the demand. The parent in this case can be considered as a factory for this small kid. Think from a parent's point of view now. The parent can make the toy himself, or he can purchase the toy from a shop to make the kid happy.

Computer World Example

Suppose your application needs to connect to different databases, such as Oracle, MySQL, or Microsoft's SQL Server. In this scenario, you may use this pattern.

In fact, this pattern is common to software applications. **You must note that the Simple Factory pattern is not treated as a standard design pattern in GoF's famous book, but the approach is common to any application you write. The idea is simple: separate the code that changes a lot from the part of the code that does not change often.** You are assumed to follow this approach in all the applications you write.

POINT TO NOTE

One of the key object-oriented design principles is to identify what varies and separate it from what does not vary.

I hope you have gotten some idea about factories. Let's separate the varying part of the previous program (Demonstration 1) in the upcoming demonstration (Demonstration 2).

Demonstration 2

First, I created another class library project, called SimpleFactoryLibrary, and added a file, called SimpleVehicleFactory.cs. This file also reuses the VehicleLibrary. Now you'll see that the SimpleVehicleFactory class exposes the public method CreateVehicle to create the objects. Here is the content:

```
// SimpleVehicleFactory.cs

using VehicleLibrary;

namespace SimpleFactoryLibrary
{
    static public class SimpleVehicleFactory
    {
        public static Vehicle? CreateVehicle(string type)
        {
            Vehicle? vehicle = null;
            if (type == "car")
            {
                vehicle = new Car();
            }
            if (type == "motorcycle")
```

```
        {
            vehicle = new Motorcycle();
        }
        return vehicle;
    }
  }
}
```

Congratulations! You have created a factory class!

Let me show you the client code (**FP_Demo2_Client.cs**) now. This time, it is very concise (notice the CreateAndDisplayVehicle method and the key change in bold):

// FP_Demo2_Client.cs

```
using VehicleLibrary;
using SimpleFactoryLibrary;
using static System.Console;

WriteLine("Using the simple factory pattern.\n");

Vehicle? vehicle = CreateAndDisplayVehicle("car");
WriteLine($"The {vehicle} construction process is completed.");

WriteLine("-----------");

vehicle = CreateAndDisplayVehicle("motorcycle");
WriteLine($"The {vehicle} construction process is completed.");

static Vehicle? CreateAndDisplayVehicle(string type)
{
    Vehicle? vehicle = SimpleVehicleFactory.CreateVehicle(type);
    vehicle?.Display();
    return vehicle;
}
```

Output

Once you execute the program, you'll see that, except for the first line, everything is identical to the previous output. I made this change to highlight that I followed the Simple Factory pattern in this demonstration. Here is the output for your ready reference:

Using the simple factory pattern.

```
A car is created.
The car construction process is completed.
-----------
A motorcycle is created.
The motorcycle construction process is completed.
```

Analysis

You can see that you separated the part that creates vehicles from the part that does not vary. This is why the following lines are still present in the CreateAndDisplayVehicle method:

```
vehicle?.Display();
return vehicle;
```

As a result, in the future, if there is any change required in the creation process, you need to change only in the SimpleVehicleFactory class (more specifically, inside the CreateVehicle method), but this client code need not be changed because of those changes.

Q&A Session

Q1.2 In this example, the clients delegate the object's creation through the Simple Factory pattern. Instead, they could directly create the objects with the new operator. Is this correct?

No. Let me remind you that one of the key object-oriented design principles is to separate the parts of your code that are most likely to change from the rest. As a result, you have the following benefits:

- In the future, if there is any change required in the creation process, you do not need to change the client code (FP_Demo2_Client.cs).

- You can avoid putting the if-else blocks (or switch statements) inside the client code. They can make your client code clumsy.

- How you are creating the objects is hidden inside the client code (FP_Demo2_Client.cs). This kind of abstraction promotes security.

- Sometimes, the life-cycle management of the created objects must be centralized to ensure consistent behavior within the application. That cannot be done if the client is free to create a concrete object the way he wishes.

Q1.3 At the end, instead of using the new operator inside the client code, you used it inside the CreateVehicle method. However, use of the new operator is very common, and no one restricts us from using it inside the client code. Isn't it correct?

Each program is indeed different, and technically, there is no problem when you use the new operator to instantiate an object. However, the designing of a program/software is important. If you read our discussion sequentially, it's easy to understand that I was trying to improve the program to accommodate the future changes in a better way.

For example, in the first program (Demonstration 1) of this chapter, if you need to consider a new type of vehicle, you must open the CreateAndDisplay Vehicle method, and you'll make the changes. This process violates the Open-Closed principle (which basically says that a code module should be open for extension, but closed for modification) of the SOLID principles.

12

Author's note: The SOLID principles were promoted by Robert C. Martin. There are many online sources that explain the concept. I also discussed these principles in detail in my other book: *Simple and Efficient Programming with C#*. However, for a quick introduction about them, you can follow the link `https://en.wikipedia.org/wiki/SOLID`. If interested, you can learn more from the following links as well: Clean Coder - Getting a SOLID start `https://sites.google.com/site/unclebobconsultingllc/getting-a-solid-start` and Clean Coder Blog.

Q1.4 However, in Demonstration 2, I still need to open the CreateVehicle method to consider new vehicles. Is this correct?

In Demonstration 2, the `CreateAndDisplayVehicle` was the only method that used the factory method. In other words, you have seen only one client of `SimpleVehicleFactory`. However, the SimpleVehicleFactory class can have many more clients who would like to use its `CreateVehicle` method.

By encapsulating the creational process in one class, you allow only one place to accommodate the upcoming changes. In fact, we already closed the `CreateAndDisplayVehicle` method for modification in Demonstration 2.

Q1.5 Why did you make the factory class static?

I took the opportunity because C# allows this. However, you may not have this facility in other programming languages. For example, in Java, you are not allowed to tag the word `static` with a top-level class. By design, the compiler will always complain about the top-level static classes in Java.

It is also true that while using a static class, you must obey certain restrictions. For example, you cannot inherit them, and so on. However, in .NET, a static outer class is not a problem, and it is quite helpful when you deep dive into functional programming using extension methods. It can make sense when you deal with some value objects that do not have an implementation class or a separate interface. It is also useful when you work with immutable classes and your factory class doesn't need to return a brand-new object each time you use it.

However, I also acknowledge that many developers do not vote for static factory classes because they are promoters for global states which are not ideal for object-oriented programming. At the end, it's a choice.

Author's note: A value object is an object whose equality is based on the values rather than the identity. The most important characteristic of a value object is that it is immutable without an identity. A simple real-life example can be given using five-rupee currency notes and five-rupee coins in India. Their money values are the same, but they are different instances.

Factory Method Implementation

The Gang of Four (GoF) mentioned the intent of the Factory Method pattern as follows:

> *Define an interface for creating an object, but let subclasses decide which class to instantiate. Factory Method lets a class defer instantiation to subclasses.*

You can see that the GoF provides some additional suggestions for making a factory in which the subclasses handle the details. What is the benefit? Let's investigate.

Each program is made based on certain assumptions. In our case, let us make the following assumptions:

- The company wants to expand its business and wants to make sports vehicles along with traditional vehicles.

- However, the current location does not have enough space. So, the company segregates the activity in different locations: in one location, it continues making traditional cars and motorcycles. And, in the other location, it starts making sports cars and sports motorcycles. In short, now the company functions with multiple factories (a.k.a. branches) at different locations.

- It is safe to assume that the company will not change its core production process to maintain its reputation and the quality of the vehicles. (In programming terminology, **you must keep the common code in one place and use it from that place to avoid code duplication**.)

This is why for the upcoming program, now I introduce a new inheritance hierarchy where you'll see three classes: VehicleFactory, TraditionalFactory, and SportsFactory. The first one is an abstract class and contains the common code. The other classes inherit from this class and make vehicles based on their preferences.

Note   To reuse the code, I have stored these classes inside a class library project, called FactoryMethodLibrary.

Let us see the abstract class (that contains the common code) with the important segment in bold:

```
using VehicleLibrary;

namespace FactoryMethodLibrary
{
    public abstract class VehicleFactory
    {
        public Vehicle? CreateAndDisplayVehicle(string type)
        {
            Vehicle? vehicle;
            vehicle = CreateVehicle(type);
            vehicle?.Display();
            return vehicle;
        }
}
```

```
    // This is the "factory method". Notice that I defer the
    //  instantiation process to the subclasses.
    protected abstract Vehicle? CreateVehicle(string type);
  }
}
```

You can see the CreateVehicle method is abstract now (I used the protected modifier to enforce that only the same class and the derived class can access this member). So, a subclass of VehicleFactory must implement this method. Once you get the vehicle from the company, the CreateAndDisplayVehicle method will invoke the Display method to display the product (this is the common code for the vehicles).

I already told you that the VehicleFactory class has two subclasses: TraditionalFactory and SportsFactory. Let's see the TraditionalFactory class:

// TraditionalFactory.cs

```
using VehicleLibrary;

namespace FactoryMethodLibrary
{
    public class TraditionalFactory : VehicleFactory
    {
        protected override Vehicle? CreateVehicle(string type)
         {
            Vehicle? vehicle = null;
            if (type == "car")
            {
                vehicle = new TraditionalCar();
            }
            if (type == "motorcycle")
            {
```

```
            vehicle = new TraditionalMotorcycle();
        }
        return vehicle;
    }
  }
}
```

Now see the SportsFactory class that is also based on the abstract VehicleFactory class:

// Sports1Factory.cs

```
using VehicleLibrary;

namespace FactoryMethodLibrary
{
    public class SportsFactory : VehicleFactory
    {
        protected override Vehicle? CreateVehicle(string type)
        {
            Vehicle? vehicle = null;
            if (type == "car")
            {
                vehicle = new SportsCar();
            }
            if (type == "motorcycle")
            {
                vehicle = new SportsMotorcycle();
            }
            return vehicle;
        }
    }
}
```

To make things easy, let's see the class diagram (Figure 1-2) of the inheritance hierarchy in the FactoryMethodLibrary as well.

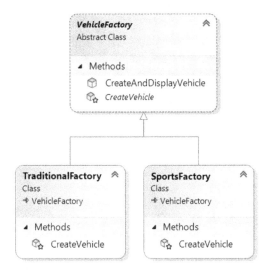

Figure 1-2. *The TraditionalFactory and SportsFactory class inherit from the VehicleFactory class*

Congratulations once again! You have implemented the factory following the GoF way, where the concrete factories create the vehicles that are instances of TraditionalCar, TraditionalMotorcycle, SportsCar, and SportsMotorcycle. Let's see one of them:

// TraditionalCar.cs

```
using static System.Console;
using VehicleLibrary;

namespace FactoryMethodLibrary
{
    internal class TraditionalCar : Vehicle
    {
        public TraditionalCar()
```

```
    {
        type = "traditional car";
    }

    public override void Display()
    {
        WriteLine($"A {this} is created.");
    }
    public override string ToString()
    {
        return type;
    }
  }
}
```

You can see that the TraditionalCar class inherits from the Vehicle class. So, I reused VehicleLibrary here as well.

Now see another class: TraditionalMotorcycle. This class is very similar. It is as follows:

// TraditionalMotorcycle.cs

```
using VehicleLibrary;
using static System.Console;

namespace FactoryMethodLibrary
{
    internal class TraditionalMotorcycle : Vehicle
    {
        public TraditionalMotorcycle()
        {
            type = "traditional motorcycle";
        }
```

```
        public override void Display()
        {
            WriteLine($"A {this} is created.");
        }
        public override string ToString()
        {
            return type;
        }
    }
}
```

Since the SportsCar and SportsMotorcycle are also very similar, I do not show them here. You can download the complete code from the Apress website. However, to make things easy for you, let me show you the class diagram (see Figure 1-3).

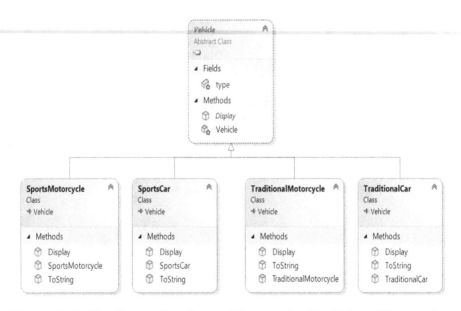

Figure 1-3. *The SportsCar, SportsMotorcycle, TraditionalCar, and TraditionalMotorcycle classes inherit from the Vehicle class*

Demonstration 3

Let's see the client code (**FP_Demo3_Client.cs**) now:

// FP_Demo3_Client.cs

```
using static System.Console;
using FactoryMethodLibrary;
using VehicleLibrary;

WriteLine("The Factory Method pattern demonstration.\n");

VehicleFactory factory;

factory = new SportsFactory();
Vehicle? vehicle = factory.CreateAndDisplayVehicle("car");
WriteLine($"The {vehicle} construction process is completed.");
WriteLine("-----------");
vehicle = factory.CreateAndDisplayVehicle("motorcycle");
WriteLine($"The {vehicle} construction process is completed.");

WriteLine("\n===================");

factory = new TraditionalFactory();
vehicle=factory.CreateAndDisplayVehicle("car");
WriteLine($"The {vehicle} construction process is completed.");
WriteLine("-----------");
vehicle=factory.CreateAndDisplayVehicle("motorcycle");
WriteLine($"The {vehicle} construction process is completed.");
```

Output

Once you execute the program, you'll see the following output:

```
The Factory Method pattern demonstration.
```

```
A sports car is created.
The sports car construction process is completed.
-----------
A sports motorcycle is created.
The sports motorcycle construction process is completed.

====================
A traditional car is created.
The traditional car construction process is completed.
-----------
A traditional motorcycle is created.
The traditional motorcycle construction process is completed.
```

Q&A Session

Q1.6 What are the advantages of using a factory like this?

Here are some key advantages:

- You are separating the code that varies from the code that does not vary (in other words, the advantages of using the Simple Factory pattern are still present). This helps you to maintain the code easily.

- The code is not tightly coupled. As a result, you can add new vehicles and/or delete existing vehicles without modifying the existing architecture. In other words, we have followed the "Open-Closed" principle.

- A client can use a factory method without knowing how the actual type of object is created.

Q1.7 You should always mark the factory method with an abstract keyword so that subclasses can complete it. Is this correct?

No. Sometimes you may be interested in a default factory method if the creator has no subclasses. In that case, you cannot mark the factory method with an abstract keyword.

However, to see the real power of the Factory Method pattern, you may need to follow the design that is implemented here in most cases.

Q1.8 The pattern used in Demonstration 3 supports two parallel hierarchies. Is this correct?

Good catch. Yes, from the class diagrams, it is evident that this pattern supports parallel class hierarchies; I've marked them in Figure 1-4.

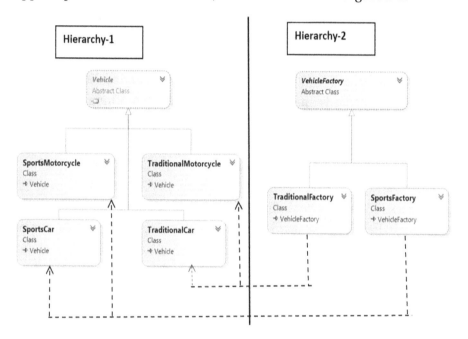

Figure 1-4. *The different inheritance hierarchies in this example*

POINT TO NOTE

In Figure 1-4, I used the dashed arrowhead lines to show which classes instantiate which others. The arrow points to the class that is instantiated. It's similar to the GoF book that used the OMT (Object Modeling Technique) notions. However, in the GoF book, the end arrow was filled. Since OMT didn't support this notion, they introduced that diagram to show this kind of relationship and named it "creates" relationship.

You can notice that the creators and their creations/products are forming separate hierarchies that are running in parallel.

Q1.9 Can you discuss more about the difference between Simple Factory and Factory Method patterns?

You should not forget the key aim of the Factory Method pattern; it is supplying you with the framework through which different subclasses can make different products. In the case of the Simple Factory pattern, you cannot similarly vary the products. You can think of the Simple Factory pattern as a one-time deal, but most importantly, your creational part will not be closed for modification. Whenever you want to represent something new, you need to add some code into the `if-else` block (or a `switch` statement) in the factory class of your Simple Factory pattern.

In this context, remember the GoF definition, which says that the Factory Method pattern lets a class defer instantiation to subclasses. In Demonstration 3, the `CreateVehicle` method was used to create a vehicle using the subclasses of `VehicleFactory`. It is the factory method that was "abstract" by design. When the `CreateAndDisplayVehicle` method used the `CreateVehicle` method inside its body, it had no clue whether it would work on a car or a motorcycle. The subclasses of `VehicleFactory` only know how to create the concrete implementations (a car or a motorcycle) for this application.

Let's revise how a client used these factories as shown in the diagrams. Figure 1-5 shows how the client used the Simple Factory pattern.

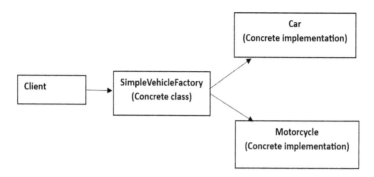

Figure 1-5. *The workflow in Demonstration 2 that uses the Simple Factory pattern*

Figure 1-6 shows how the client used the Factory Method pattern.

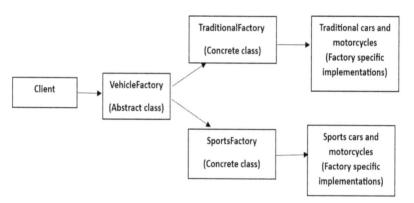

Figure 1-6. *The workflow in Demonstration 3 that uses the Factory Method pattern*

25

CHAPTER 2

Singleton Pattern

The Singleton pattern can be implemented in many ways. Each approach has its pros and cons. You'll see four different approaches in this chapter.

Concept

The Gang of Four (GoF) defined the intent of the Singleton pattern as follows:

> *Ensure a class only has one instance, and provide a global point of access to it.*

Let's assume you have a class named `Sample`, and you need to create an object from it. Normally, what would you do? You guessed it right; you can simply use the following line of code: `Sample sample = new();`.

But let's see it closely. If you keep using the "new" keyword ten more times, you'll have ten more objects. Right? But in a real-world scenario, unnecessary object creation is a big concern (particularly when constructor calls are costly), and we need to restrict this. In a situation like this, the Singleton pattern comes into the picture. It restricts the use of the new operator and ensures that you do not have more than one instance of the class.

In short, this pattern says that a particular class should have only one instance. If an instance is unavailable, you can create one; otherwise, you should use an existing one to serve your needs.

© Vaskaran Sarcar 2025
V. Sarcar, *Creational Design Patterns in C#*, Apress Pocket Guides,
https://doi.org/10.1007/979-8-8688-1567-6_2

Real-Life Example

Let's assume you have a sports team, and the team is participating in a tournament. Your team needs to play against multiple opponents throughout the tournament. At the beginning of each of these matches, as per the game's rules, the captains of the two sides must go for a coin toss. So, if your team does not have a captain, you need to elect someone as a captain first. Before each game and each coin toss, you do not repeat the process of electing a captain if you have already nominated a person as a captain of your team for this tournament. In this example, selecting a captain is like creating a new object. Having that captain for the rest of the season is like reusing the same object that was created at the beginning.

Computer World Example

In some software systems, you may decide to maintain only one file system so that you can use it for the centralized management of resources. This approach can help you implement caching mechanisms effectively. This pattern can also be used to maintain a thread pool in a multithreading environment.

Implementation

The first demonstration shows a simple approach to model a singleton class, named Captain. This class has a private constructor that prevents you from instantiating this class outside. So, inside the client code, you cannot write something like the following:

```
Captain captain = new();  // Inaccessible
```

Since the class is sealed, you cannot write something like the following as well:

```
class Derived : Captain { }  // Error
```

Note   Since I already had the private constructor, I could avoid using the sealed keyword in this demonstration. Then why did I make the class sealed? It can be beneficial if you make some specific modifications. You'll see a discussion on this in Q2.1.

How can you get an instance of the Captain class? You guessed it right: you can opt for a utility method or a property. In this example, I chose a property. So, in my singleton class, you'll see the following code (to shorten the code, you can use the compound assignment using the null coalescing operator; I have shown it in the commented code):

```
get
{
    if (_instance == null)
    {
        _instance = new();
    }
    //_instance ??= new(); // Compound assignment
    return _instance;
}
```

Finally, there is a field called status. I used it to show whether there is any instance of the Captain class being created. Let's see the complete class now (I kept some supportive comments for your easy understanding):

Note   Earlier, Microsoft recommended Pascal naming conventions for static fields (see Static Field Naming Guidelines I Microsoft Learn). However, Identifier names - rules and conventions - C# I Microsoft Learn suggests that you start with s_. Again, the following link Names of Type Members - Framework Design Guidelines I Microsoft Learn states that do not use "g_" or "s_" to indicate static fields.

To avoid the confusion, I'll simplify things by following Pascal naming conventions for public properties and using an underscore as a prefix for the private fields (static or non-static).

// Captain.cs

```
using static System.Console;

#region Approach-1: Not OK for multithreaded environment
sealed class Captain
{
    readonly string status = "is not elected.";
    private Captain()
    {
        status = "is ready for the coin toss.";
        WriteLine("One captain is elected for the team.");
    }

    private static Captain? _instance;
    public static Captain Instance
    {
        get
        {
            if (_instance == null)
            {
                _instance = new();
            }
            // Or, use a compound assignment
            //_instance ??= new();
            return _instance;
        }
    }
}
```

```
    public string GetStatus() => status;
}
#endregion
```

Before you see the client code, let's visualize the class diagram of this
Captain class (see Figure 2-1) as well.

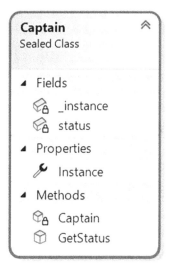

Figure 2-1. *Class diagram of the Captain class*

Visual Studio's Class Designer tool allows you to show associations
in the class diagram. Using this feature, I can alternatively present the
Captain class as shown in Figure 2-2.

Figure 2-2. *The _instance field is shown as an association in the class diagram of the Captain class*

Demonstration 1

Let's use the Captain class now. When you download the source code from the Apress website, you can see the client code inside SP_Demo1_Client.cs.

// SP_Demo1_Client.cs

```
using static System.Console;

Captain captain1 = Captain.Instance;
WriteLine($"The captain {captain1.GetStatus()}");
Captain captain2 = Captain.Instance;
WriteLine($"The captain {captain2.GetStatus()}");
```

Output

Upon executing this program, you'll get the following output:

```
One captain is elected for the team.
```

The captain is ready for the coin toss.
The captain is ready for the coin toss.

Analysis

In the client code, you tried to get two instances (captain1 and captain2) of the Captain class. However, you can see that the captain is elected only once. **Congratulations! You have learned to model a Singleton pattern.**

   However, this model may not work in a multithreaded environment. To illustrate, let me replace the following block of code:

```
Captain captain1 = Captain.Instance;
WriteLine($"The captain {captain1.GetStatus()}");
Captain captain2 = Captain.Instance;
WriteLine($"The captain {captain2.GetStatus()}");
```

   with the following one:

```
#region Discussing the problem in a multithreaded environment

Captain captain;
var task1 = Task.Run(
  () =>
  {
   captain = Captain.Instance;
   WriteLine($"The captain {captain.GetStatus()}");
  }
  );

var task2 = Task.Run(
  () =>
  {
   captain = Captain.Instance;
```

```
  WriteLine($"The captain {captain.GetStatus()}");
 }
);
Task.WaitAll(task1, task2);
#endregion
```

After making this change, once I executed the program again, I could see the following output on my computer (let me remind you that you may or may not not see the same output because you are now executing the code in a multi-threaded environment):

```
One captain is elected for the team.
One captain is elected for the team.
The captain is ready for the coin toss.
The captain is ready for the coin toss.
```

In this output, you can see the line "One captain is elected for the team." twice. It indicates that both tasks were able to create a Captain instance. So, let us improve our model in the next demonstration.

Q&A Session

Q2.1 Since the Captain class already included the private constructor, I do not see the need to use the sealed keyword. Is this correct?

Let us exercise a program, where the Captain class is **not** sealed, and you add a nested class (NestedDerived) inside the Captain class as follows:

```
//sealed class Captain
class Captain
{
    readonly string status = "is not elected.";
    private Captain()
    {
        status = "is ready for the coin toss.";
```

```
        WriteLine("One captain is elected for the team.");
    }
    private static Captain? _instance;
    public static Captain Instance
    {
        get
        {
            //if (_instance == null)
            //{
            //    _instance = new();
            //}
            // Or, use a compound assignment
            _instance ??= new();
            return _instance;
        }
    }

    public string GetStatus() => status;

    #region This code block is added to discuss the Q&A
    public class NestedDerived : Captain
    {
        // Some other code, if any
    }
    #endregion

}
```

Now, let a client exercise the following code:

```
#region Discussing the problem without the sealed keyword

Captain.NestedDerived derived1 = new();
Captain.NestedDerived derived2 = new();

#endregion
```

Once you execute the program, you'll see the following output:

```
One captain is elected for the team.
One captain is elected for the team.
```

You can see that each time you instantiate the **Captain.NestedDerived** class, it elects a captain. Now you understand that by marking the Captain class sealed, you can avoid the misuse of the singleton class through a nested class.

Q2.2 Why are multiple object creations a big concern?

Here are some important points that you can remember:

- Object creations in the real world can be costly if you work with resource-intensive objects.

- In some cases, the creation of objects is time-consuming, and it may not be a one-step process (you will learn more about this in the **Builder** pattern in Chapter 3.)

- In some applications, you may need to pass a common object to multiple places.

Alternative Implementations

You have already seen an example and understood that it is not suitable for a multithreaded environment. So, let us improve the previous implementation.

Demonstration 2

You have seen that in a multithreaded environment, multiple threads can examine the if condition simultaneously. As a result, they may create multiple instances of the Captain class. So, let us guard the problem using a lock statement. Here is a sample implementation (notice the key changes in bold):

```
// There is no change in the client code
#region Approach-2: Can work in a multithreaded environment
class Captain
{
    readonly string status = "is not elected yet";
    private Captain()
    {
        status = "is ready for the coin toss.";
        WriteLine("One captain is elected for the team.");
    }
    private static readonly object _lock = new();
    private static Captain? _instance;
    public static Captain Instance
    {
        get
        {
            lock (_lock)
            {
                _instance ??= new();
            }
            return _instance;
        }
    }

    public string GetStatus() => status;
}
#endregion
```

Let's use the previous client code and execute the program again.

```
                         POINT TO NOTE
```

In all these different approaches, the client code is essentially the same. For
brevity, I did not add this segment repeatedly in these discussions. However,
you can download the full implementations from the Apress website.

Output

This time, you'll see the following output:

```
One captain is elected for the team.
The captain is ready for the coin toss.
The captain is ready for the coin toss.
```

Analysis

You can see that the program is showing the expected behavior by electing
the captain only once, and each time, this captain was ready for the
coin toss. This is a common approach to model a Singleton pattern. By
downloading the project **SP_Demo2_UsingLock** from the Apress website,
you can execute the complete program.

However, by imposing a lock, you promote a blocking operation (and
add an additional overhead) in your program. In addition, debugging
becomes tricky while the code deals with locks. These are some of the
reasons that encourage you to search for a lock-free implementation. Let
us examine this in the upcoming demonstration.

Author's note: In my other book, *Design Patterns in C#* (Second Edition),
I used double-checked locking. However, to make the code simple, I used
only one lock statement here.

Demonstration 3

In this implementation, you write concise code. Here, you instantiate the Captain class when you call the Instance property for the first time (i.e., you can say that it is one type of lazy initialization). Here is the code with the key changes in bold:

```
#region Approach-3: Concise implementation
sealed class Captain
{
    readonly string status = "is not elected yet";
    private Captain()
    {
        status = "is ready for the coin toss.";
        WriteLine("One captain is elected for the team.");
    }
    private static readonly Captain _instance = new();
    public static Captain Instance
    {
        get { return _instance; }
    }

    public string GetStatus() => status;

}
#endregion
```

Output

If you use this Captain class in any of the previous demonstrations, you'll see the same output (that you saw in Demonstration 2). This kind of coding is often termed **static initialization**.

Analysis

This approach still has the following pros and cons:

Pros

- This approach is straightforward and cleaner.
- It is thread-safe.
- It offers some sort of lazy initialization (full laziness will be achieved in the next demonstration).

Cons

- You may see an unwanted output.

To examine this point, let us add a dummy variable (Flag) at the end of the singleton class as follows:

```
using static System.Console;
```

```
#region Approach-3: Concise implementation
sealed class Captain
{
    // There is no change in the previous code
     public string GetStatus() => status;

     #region To discuss the problem of this approach
     public static int Flag = 2;
     #endregion
}
```

Now use the following client code:

```
#region Discussing the problem of Approach-3
WriteLine(Captain.Flag);
#endregion
```

Once you run this program, you'll see the following output:

```
One captain is elected for the team.
2
```

You can notice that the program elected a captain before it shows the value of the variable. However, you did not have any intention to elect a captain at this point. So, you have less control over the instantiation process.

Demonstration 4

Let me show you another approach using advanced built-in constructs in C#. I'll use the Lazy<T> class and delegates (or lambda expressions) this time. Let me explain a few points before you see the new look of the Captain class.

The Lazy<T> class is used to support lazy initialization. At the time of this writing, it has seven different public constructors. Here is a Visual Studio snapshot for you (see Figure 2-3).

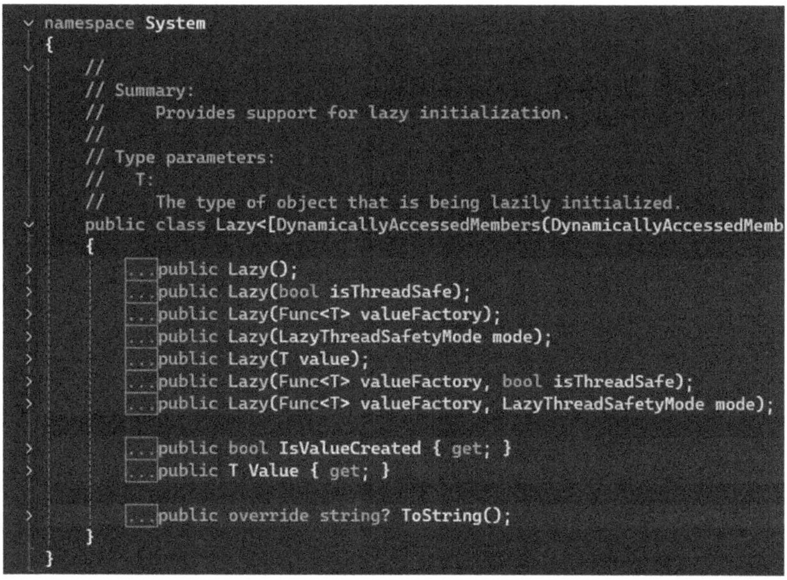

Figure 2-3. *Visual Studio snapshot for the Lazy<T> class*

In the upcoming model, my focus was on the following version (I have kept the remark that shows its usefulness as well):

```
/// <remarks>
/// An instance created with this constructor may be used
/// concurrently from multiple threads.
/// </remarks>
public Lazy(Func<T> valueFactory);
```

So, I used the following code:

```
private static readonly Lazy<Captain> _instance = new(
  () => new Captain()
);
```

The Value property is used to retrieve the lazily initialized value of the current Lazy<T> instance. This is why you'll see the following code:

```
public static Captain Instance
{
    get { return _instance.Value; }
}
```

Now you should not have any trouble understanding the new look of the Captain class with the key changes in bold (I have kept the previous code for your ready reference):

```
#region Approach-4: Lazy Initialization
sealed class Captain
{
    readonly string status = "is not elected yet";
    private Captain()
    {
        status = "is ready for the coin toss.";
```

```
        WriteLine("One captain is elected for the team.");
    }
    // private static readonly Captain _instance = new();
    private static readonly Lazy<Captain> _instance = new(
        () => new Captain()
    );

    public static Captain Instance
    {
        // get { return _instance; }
        get { return _instance.Value; }
    }

    public string GetStatus() => status;
}
#endregion
```

Output

If you use this Captain class in any of the previous demonstrations, you'll see the same and expected output where the captain is elected only once.

As said before, there are many approaches for modeling a Singleton design pattern. You have already seen some of the popular approaches in this chapter. So, I believe that now you have an idea of how to model a Singleton pattern for your application.

Q&A Session

Q2.3 What do you mean by the term "Lazy initialization?
It's a technique that you use to delay the object creation process. The basic idea is you should create the object only when it is truly required. This approach is useful when object creation is a costly operation for you.

Q2.4 When should I use the Singleton pattern?

Here are some common use cases where you'll find this pattern useful:

- To work with a centralized system (e.g., consider a database)

- To maintain a common log file

- To maintain a thread pool in a multithreaded environment

- To implement a caching mechanism or device drivers

Q2.5 I have seen many debates on modeling Singleton patterns. I'd like to know your thoughts on those.

True. In fact, "performance vs. laziness" is always a concern in this pattern, and some developers always question those areas. Still, I believe that you will find this pattern helpful while building real-world applications. You may not like to use it very often, but its usefulness in certain scenarios is inevitable. In this context, I'd like you to visit the online link https://www.informit.com/articles/article.aspx?p=1404056&lang=en that shows the following Erich Gamma quote, which came in an interview in 2009:

> *When discussing which patterns to drop, we found that we still love them all. (Not really—I'm in favor of dropping Singleton. Its use is almost always a design smell.)*

For me, this quote is applicable in 2025 as well!

CHAPTER 3

Builder Pattern

The Builder pattern is useful for creating complex objects that have multiple parts. The Gang of Four (GoF) defined the intent of this pattern as follows:

> *Separate the construction of a complex object from its representation so that the same construction process can create different representations.*

This pattern may be difficult to understand on the first attempt. However, once you analyze the code snippets and examples, the topic will become easier.

Concept

The first thing to remember is that the Builder pattern does not deal with single-step creations. Instead, it uses a configurable sequence of steps to make a complex object. You can reuse a specific process to build the products as well. As per the classical GoF book, four players are involved in this pattern. Let me summarize them as follows:

- **Product**: It is a complex object that has many parts. In this chapter, you are about to construct cars using this pattern.

© Vaskaran Sarcar 2025
V. Sarcar, *Creational Design Patterns in C#*, Apress Pocket Guides,
https://doi.org/10.1007/979-8-8688-1567-6_3

- **Builder**: It provides the abstract interface for creating parts of the complex object, i.e., the `Product` object.

- **ConcreteBuilder**: By implementing the `Builder` interface, it creates and assembles different parts of the product and provides an interface for retrieving it.

- **Director**: It constructs the object using the `Builder` interface.

Let me clear the roles using the following examples.

Real-Life Example

A car manufacturing company can produce different cars, such as traditional (a.k.a. regular) cars and electric cars. It manufactures different parts of these cars and later assembles those parts as per the model's specifications. You must agree that this is a complex process. In addition, these parts are specific to the type of vehicle. So, the company can make two units, say a traditional car builder unit and an electrical car builder unit, to make these cars. Since these two units work differently, it is no wonder that a traditional (a.k.a. regular) car looks different from an electric car. Finally, there must be someone who supervises the overall process and instructs the units on how to make the cars. In this example, you can consider a car as the final `Product`, each car builder unit as a `ConcreteBuilder`, and the company supervisor as the `Director`.

Let's consider another example. To complete an order for a computer, different hardware parts can be assembled based on customer preferences. For example, a customer can opt for a 1000GB hard disk with an Intel processor. If there is a budget constraint, another customer can choose a 500GB hard disk with an AMD processor. Here, the computer is the final `Product`, the customer plays the role of the `Director`, and the seller/assembler plays the role of the `ConcreteBuilder`.

Computer World Example

The classical GoF book considers an example when a typical application tries to convert one text format to another text format, such as converting from Rich Text Format (RTF) to ASCII text. A similar example is very common when you see online converters convert a Word (.docx) document to a PDF file (.pdf) or a plain text (.txt).

While programming similar examples, at a high level, you can think of a reader and a converter where the reader parses the document and the converter converts the document to a target format using a specialized converter. So, the converter can have specialized subclasses, such as an ASCII text converter, PDF converter, or TXT converter, to perform these conversions. In this example, the converter plays the role of a Builder, the specialized converters (such as PDF converters or TXT converters) play the role of ConcreteBuilder, the Word doc reader plays the role of a Director, and a converted file (such as .PDF or .TXT) is the final Product.

These examples give you a clue when to use the Builder pattern. So, let me summarize the points.

- You'd like to create a complex object that has many parts.

- Constructions of these parts are independent of each other.

- Constructions of these parts are also independent of how they are assembled.

- The pattern is useful when the construction process allows you to create different representations of the object.

Implementation

In our upcoming example, you are about to create different cars. So, the Car class represents the Product. The Builder class defines all possible methods to construct a car. The ElectricCarBuilder and TraditionalCarBuilder are concrete classes that inherit from this Builder class.

A client creates a Director object and configures it with a Builder object to make the cars. For example, the director uses the TraditionalCarBuilder instances to construct and assemble parts of a traditional car. Similarly, the director can use the ElectricCarBuilder instances to construct an electric car.

Let's see the Car class:

```csharp
using static System.Console;
// The Car class represents the "Product"
class Car
{
    /*
     * You can use any data structure that you prefer.
     * I have used LinkedList<String> in this case.
     */

    private LinkedList<string> _parts;
    private string _type;
    public Car(string type)
    {
        _type = type;
        _parts = new LinkedList<string>();
    }
}
```

```
public int HeadLights { get; set; }
public string Motor { get; set; }
public int Wheels { get; set; }
// By default, the exhaust emission system is not needed
// for an electric car
public string ExhaustEmissions{ get; set; } = "not set";
public void Add(string part)
{
    // Adding parts
    _parts.AddLast(part);
}

public void ShowProduct()
{
    WriteLine($"The {_type} car construction sequence:");
    foreach (string part in _parts)
        WriteLine(part);
}
}
```

PRIMARY CONSTRUCTOR MAKES THE CODE CONCISE

Using the Primary constructor (introduced in C#12) and removing the _type field, you can make the Car class concise as follows:

```
#region The code segment that uses a primary constructor
```

class Car(string type)

```
{
    /*

    * You can use any data structure that you prefer.
```

```
    * I have used LinkedList<String> in this case.

    */

    private LinkedList<string> _parts = new();

    // There are no other changes in the remaining code

#endregion
```

You can make similar changes in equivalent code as well. I showed you the code with and without primary constructors to make you familiar with both approaches. Sometimes I avoid writing code that is very specific to the C# programming language because many C# developers are Java developers as well. In fact, the preface of the classical GoF book says that **the design patterns require neither unusual language features nor amazing programming tricks with which to astound your friends and managers**. However, you can have a different thought. So, you can choose the approach that serves you best.

Typically, a builder interface is needed for creating parts of a Product object. In our example, **Builder** is an abstract class that plays this role. It contains the methods to build different parts of a product.

In this example, you see an empty method, called AddExhaustSystem, in the Builder class. Why? Ideally, this class should define all possible methods to build various parts of a product (in our example, a car). We can assume that an electric car does not need an exhaust emission system, whereas a traditional car must have such a component. I could make other methods in the Builder class empty as well; however, I forced the concrete builders to implement those methods.

There is another method, called GetCar, in this class. This method retrieves the product once the parts are assembled. Let's have a look at this class now:

```
abstract class Builder
{
    public abstract void SetMotor();
    public abstract void InsertWheels();
    public abstract void SetHeadlights();
    // The exhaust emissions system is needed for regular cars
    public virtual void AddExhaustSystem() { }
    // To retrieve the constructed product.
    public abstract Car GetCar();
}
```

In the upcoming examples, the **TraditionalCarBuilder** and **ElectricCarBuilder** classes make the traditional cars and electric cars, respectively. In other words, these are the concrete builders that build the internal representations of a Car instance. First, see the **ElectricCarBuilder** class:

```
// The ElectricCarBuilder builds electric cars.

class ElectricCarBuilder : Builder
{
    private readonly Car _car;
    public ElectricCarBuilder()
    {
        _car = new("electric");
    }
    public override void SetMotor()
    {
        _car.Motor = "electric motors and batteries";
        _car.Add($"The {_car.Motor} are added.");
    }
```

```
public override void InsertWheels()
{
    _car.Wheels = 4;
    _car.Add($"{_car.Wheels} wheels are added to the car.");
}
public override void SetHeadlights()
{
    _car.HeadLights = 2;
    _car.Add($"{_car.HeadLights} headlights are set.");
}

// NOTE: The electric car does not need the exhaust
// emission system. So, we do not need to override the base
// class method.

// Retrieve the constructed car
public override Car GetCar()
{
    return _car;
}
}
```

Now see the TraditionalCarBuilder class (notice that it overrides the AddExhaustSystem method as well):

```
// The TraditionalCarBuilder builds traditional cars.

class TraditionalCarBuilder : Builder
{
    private readonly Car _car;
    public TraditionalCarBuilder()
    {
        _car = new("traditional");
    }
```

```csharp
public override void SetMotor()
{
    _car.Motor = "internal combustion engine (fueled by
    diesel)";
    _car.Add($"The {_car.Motor} is added.");
}

public override void InsertWheels()
{
    _car.Wheels = 6;
    _car.Add($"{_car.Wheels} wheels are added to the car.");
}
public override void SetHeadlights()
{
    _car.HeadLights = 4;
    _car.Add($"{_car.HeadLights} headlights are set.");
}
// NOTE: The traditional car needs to have an exhaust
// emission system. So, we need to override the base
// class method.
public override void AddExhaustSystem()
{
    _car.ExhaustEmissions = "set";
    _car.Add($"An exhaust emissions system is
       {_car.ExhaustEmissions}.");
}

// Retrieve the constructed car
public override Car GetCar()
{
    return _car;
}
}
```

The **Director** is responsible for creating the final object using the Builder interface. It is important to note that the director is the one who decides the sequence of steps to build the product. You can safely assume that a director can vary the sequence as per his wish. Here is the Director class:

```
using static System.Console;

// The director directs the steps to make the product (car).
class Director
{
    // The director performs the steps in the following
    // sequence and returns the constructed product:
    // Set motor->Insert wheels->Set headlights->Add exhaust
    // system (if applicable)
    public Car Instruct(Builder builder)
    {
        builder.SetMotor();
        builder.InsertWheels();
        builder.SetHeadlights();
        builder.AddExhaustSystem();
        return builder.GetCar();
    }
}
```

You have seen the major players of the Builder pattern. Now let me show you the class diagram (Figure 3-1) for the upcoming demonstration.

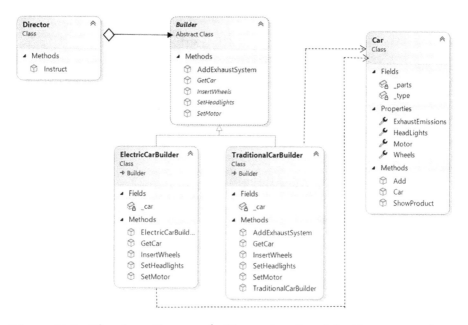

Figure 3-1. *The class diagram (without the client) for Demonstration 1 that uses the Builder pattern*

Author's note: To better understand, I have edited the class diagram that was generated by Visual Studio's Class Designer. Here, I showed the Aggregation relationship using the conventional notions. I used the dashed line(s) ending with an arrow to show which classes instantiate which others.

Demonstration 1

Let's allow a client to make some cars now:

```csharp
// BP_Demo1_Client.cs
using static System.Console;
WriteLine("*** Builder Pattern Demonstration. * **");

Director director = new();
```

```
// Making a traditional car
Builder builder = new TraditionalCarBuilder();
Car car = director.Instruct(builder);
car.ShowProduct();

WriteLine("============");
// Making an electric car now.")
builder = new ElectricCarBuilder();
car = director.Instruct(builder);
car.ShowProduct();
```

Output

Here is the output:

```
*** Builder Pattern Demonstration. * **
The traditional car construction sequence:
The internal combustion engine (fueled by diesel) is added.
6 wheels are added to the car.
4 headlights are set.
An exhaust emissions system is set.
============
The electric car construction sequence:
The electric motors and batteries are added.
4 wheels are added to the car.
2 headlights are set.
```

Analysis

While constructing the cars, in each case, I first built the cars and then showed the steps (by invoking the ShowProduct method on the car instance). In the next demonstration, you'll see me using method chaining. Then you understand that the following lines

```
Car car = director.Instruct(builder);
car.ShowProduct();
```

can be replaced with a single line as follows:

```
director.Instruct(builder).ShowProduct();
```

It indicates that there was no need to create the `Car` variable in the client code. However, this one line of additional code looks OK to me because the current structure clearly depicts how the director is building a car.

Q&A Session

Q3.1 What is the advantage of using a Builder pattern?
Here are some advantages:

- You direct the builder to build the objects step by step, and you promote encapsulation by hiding the details of the complex construction process. The director can retrieve the final product from the builder when the whole construction is over. In general, at a high level, you seem to have only one method that makes the product, but there are other internal methods that are hidden from the client. So, you have finer control over the construction process.

- Using this pattern, the same construction process can produce different products.

- In short, by changing the type of a builder, you change the internal representation of the product.

Q3.2 What are the drawbacks associated with a Builder pattern?
Here are some challenges:

- It is not suitable if you want to deal with mutable objects (which can be modified later).

- You may need to duplicate some portion of the code. These duplications may cause performance impact in some contexts.

- To create more specific products, you need to create more concrete builders.

Q3.3 Why are you using a separate class for the director? You could use the client code to play the role of the director. Is this correct?
No one restricts you from doing that. In the preceding implementation, I wanted to separate this role from the client code in the implementation. In the upcoming demonstration, I'll make the client a director.

Q3.4 I have read your other book: *Java Design Patterns* (Third Edition). In that book, you used specialized directors and specialized products as well. However, in this example, you used only specialized builders. Is there any specific thought behind this?
That is a fat book with a detailed discussion on many different topics. Yes, by making a common class (or interface) for specialized products and a common class (or interface) for specialized directors, you can make a bigger system. However, this is a pocketbook. To make the example simple, I have shown you this concise implementation. In addition, the GoF shared their thoughts as follows:

> *Why no abstract class for products? In the common case, the products produced by the concrete builders differ so greatly in their representation that there is little to gain from giving different products a common parent class.*

You can verify this quote by looking at the output of Demonstration 1 where a traditional car is very much different from an electric car.

Q3.5 If I involve more specialized directors, they can follow a different sequence of steps. Is this correct?

Yes. It is a good find. The upcoming demonstration uses method chaining to vary the steps inside the client code. It is very useful in this kind of design.

Alternative Implementation

Using **method chaining**, now I'll show you an alternative implementation. In this program, **the client will play the role of a director**. So, I need to incorporate some changes in the previous demonstration. Let's see them.

Like the previous example, Builder represents the builder interface, but now the void return type is changed to Builder as follows:

```
abstract class Builder
{
    public abstract Builder SetMotor();
    public abstract Builder InsertWheels();
    public abstract Builder SetHeadlights();
    // The charging point is needed only for the electric vehicles
    public virtual Builder AddExhaustSystem() {  return this;  }
    // To retrieve the constructed product.
    public abstract Car GetCar();
}
```

As a result, the inherited classes of the Builder class (TraditionalCarBuilder and ElectricCarBuilder) need to make some changes as well. First, see the TraditionalCarBuilder class with the key changes in bold:

```
// The TraditionalCarBuilder builds traditional cars.

class TraditionalCarBuilder : Builder
{
    private readonly Car _car;
    public TraditionalCarBuilder()
    {
        _car = new("traditional");
    }
    public override Builder SetMotor()
    {
        _car.Motor = "internal combustion engine (fueled by diesel)";
        _car.Add($"The {_car.Motor} is added.");
        return this;
    }

    public override Builder InsertWheels()
    {
        _car.Wheels = 6;
        _car.Add($"{_car.Wheels} wheels are added to the car.");
        return this;
    }
    public override Builder SetHeadlights()
    {
        _car.HeadLights = 4;
        _car.Add($"{_car.HeadLights}  headlights are set.");
        return this;
    }
}
```

```
// NOTE: The traditional car needs to have an exhaust
// emission system. So, we need to override the base
// class method.
public override Builder AddExhaustSystem()
{
    _car.ExhaustEmissions = "set";
    _car.Add($"An exhaust emissions system is {_car.
    ExhaustEmissions}.");
    return this;
}

// Retrieve the constructed car
public override Car GetCar()
{
    return _car;
}
}
```

Notice that these methods are similar to the previous demonstration, but there is one major change: their return type is Builder. Since the return type is Builder, now a client can apply **method chaining** to assemble the parts.

The ElectricCarBuilder class makes similar changes. To avoid repetition, I do not show it here.

Demonstration 2

Let's see how a client can vary the steps to make different products in the following example:

```
using System.IO;
using static System.Console;
```

```
WriteLine("*** Builder Pattern Demonstration 2.***");

// Making a traditional car
// The director performs the following steps before returning
// the product:
// Set motor->Insert wheels->Set headlights->Add exhaust system
Builder builder = new TraditionalCarBuilder();
Car car=builder.SetMotor()
    .InsertWheels()
    .SetHeadlights()
    .AddExhaustSystem()
    .GetCar();
car.ShowProduct();

WriteLine("============");
// Making an electric car now.")
// The director follows a different sequence and returns the
// constructed product:
// Set motor->Set headlights-> Insert wheels.

builder = new ElectricCarBuilder();
car = builder.SetMotor()
    .SetHeadlights()
    .InsertWheels()
    // .AddExhaustSystem() // Not required here
    .GetCar();
car.ShowProduct();
```

The Car class was unchanged during this demonstration. Since you have seen this class and the other classes already, I have only shown the client code in this demonstration. Similar to the previous demonstration, I first built the cars and then showed the steps (by invoking the ShowProduct method on the car instance). However, you are familiar with method chaining now. So, while constructing cars, inside the client code, you could avoid using the car variable by extending the chain as follows:

```
builder.SetMotor()
    .InsertWheels()
    .SetHeadlights()
    .AddExhaustSystem()
    .GetCar()
    .ShowProduct();
```

You can download the complete project (BP_Demo2) from the Apress website.

Output

The following output is slightly different from the output of Demonstration 1. This was intentional. It is because this time, while building an electric car, the client (a.k.a. director) set the headlights before adding the wheels. Here is the output:

```
*** Builder Pattern Demonstration 2***
The traditional car construction sequence:
The internal combustion engine (fueled by diesel) is added.
6 wheels are added to the car.
4  headlights are set.
An exhaust emissions system is set.
```

```
=============
```
The electric car construction sequence:
The electric motors and batteries are added.
2 headlights are set.
4 wheels are added to the car.

Analysis

Notice that the client (a.k.a. director in this example) created two different cars using the appropriate builder, and each time it followed a different sequence of steps. This approach helps you make an efficient and flexible application.

Q&A Session

Q3.6 Looks like you promoted functional programming and immutability in Demonstration 2. Is this correct?
Good catch. I must say that you are an excellent reader. By nature, the void methods are not immutable, and functional programming tries to minimize their usage to avoid side effects.

Author's note: Functional programming (FP) is a big topic. A detailed discussion on FP is beyond the scope of this book. However, if you like to explore FP using C#, you can refer to my other book: *Introducing Functional Programming Using C#*.

Q3.7 What is the key benefit associated with immutable objects?
Once constructed, they can be safely shared, and most importantly, they are thread-safe, so you save lots of synchronization costs in a multithreaded environment.

Q3.8 When should I consider using a Builder pattern?
As mentioned earlier, if you need to make a complex object that involves various steps of the construction process, and at the same time, the products need to be immutable, considering the Builder pattern is a good choice.

Let me show you its usefulness with a different example as well. Consider the following code snippet and analyze the potential difficulties. Here is a sample class A with a constructor that has many parameters:

```
class A
{

    A(int arg1, int arg2, int arg3,double arg4,B b, C c){
        // Some code to initialize
    }
    // Remaining code is skipped
}
class B { }
class C { }
```

Now go through the following points:

- Notice that the B object and the C object are parts of an A object. So, before you construct an instance of A, you need to create a B class object and a C class object. It indicates that you need to perform these steps before you use the A class constructor. The Builder pattern can help you write better code in a similar case.

- You can see that you also need to supply three integer arguments. Since these arguments are similar, understanding and using them can be challenging. In this case, to understand them, you need to refer to the code documentation. Also, you need to pass these arguments in the correct order. This is why **using a method (or a constructor) that needs too many parameters is not a recommended practice in general**. It is better if you pass a minimum number of arguments (preferably one or zero) at a time. So, the Builder pattern can be helpful here as well.

Q3.9 Why is passing too many mandatory arguments in a method or constructor not a recommended practice?

As said before, you need to understand their usage properly and then pass the arguments in the correct sequence. Apart from this, in many cases, a large number of configuration options may not be needed. For example, you saw that an electric car did not need the "exhaust emission system." It is better if you are not forced to pass an argument in such a case.

Q3.10 If this is the case, I'd use the subclassing mechanism. Isn't it?

You can do this. However, the library of subclasses can grow as you need more configuration steps. In addition, you may also note that a change in one class may force you to make a change in a related subclass. In either case, the maintenance becomes tough.

Q3.11 It appears that the Builder pattern is similar to the Factory pattern. Is this correct?

In the Factory pattern, you focused on a one-step creation process. However, you use the Builder pattern when you see a configurable sequence of steps.

POINT TO NOTE

In the future, you may like to learn about the Template method pattern. In that case, I'd like you to note that in the Builder pattern, the client/customer is the boss (you have already seen the client as a director in Demonstration 2) who controls the order of the algorithm. On the contrary, in the Template method pattern, you (or the developers) are the boss, and you have absolute control over the flow of the execution, which cannot be altered by a client.

CHAPTER 4

Prototype Pattern

The Prototype pattern provides an alternative method for instantiating objects by copying (or cloning) an instance of an existing object. This chapter explains this pattern and its usefulness with simple examples.

Concept

The Gang of Four (GoF) defined the intent of the Prototype pattern as follows:

> *Specify the kinds of objects to create using a prototypical instance, and create new objects by copying this prototype.*

If you notice the pattern's intent closely, you'll see that the core idea of this pattern is to create an object based on another object. This existing object acts as a template for the new object.

Now the question is why do we want cloning? The simple answer is that it can save time and expenses in certain situations. Here are some examples:

- You need some resources to make an instance, but these resources may not be easily available.

- The construction of a new instance from scratch is a time-consuming and costly operation.

© Vaskaran Sarcar 2025
V. Sarcar, *Creational Design Patterns in C#*, Apress Pocket Guides,
https://doi.org/10.1007/979-8-8688-1567-6_4

Real-Life Example

Suppose you have a master copy of a valuable document. You need to incorporate some change(s) to it, and then you analyze the effect of the change(s). In this case, you can make a photocopy of the original document and edit the changes in the photocopied document.

Computer World Example

Let's assume that you already have a stable application. In the future, you may want to modify the application with some minor changes. You must start with a copy of your original application, make the changes, and then analyze further. Surely you do not want to start from scratch to incorporate a minor change to save time and money.

In .NET, the ICloneable interface contains a Clone() method. You can use this built-in construct when you implement the Prototype pattern. However, the official documentation (see ICloneable Interface (System) | Microsoft Learn) warns you by saying the following:

> *It does not specify whether the cloning operation performs a deep copy, a shallow copy, or something in between. Nor does it require all property values of the original instance to be copied to the new instance. For example, the Clone() method performs a shallow copy of all properties except the IsReadOnly property; it always sets this property value to false in the cloned object. Because callers of Clone() cannot depend on the method performing a predictable cloning operation, we recommend that ICloneable not be implemented in public APIs.*

This is why I used a custom method for cloning in the upcoming program. Let me also tell you that **I'll use a deep copy in this implementation**. However, to copy some specific fields, you'll see me using the MemberwiseClone() method as well. This method is defined in the Object class and performs a shallow copy. Let me pick some information about it from the Visual Studio:

68

```
// Returns a new object instance that is a memberwise copy of
// this object. This is always a shallow copy of the instance.
// The method is protected so that other object may only call
// this method on themselves. It is intended to support the
// ICloneable interface.
[Intrinsic]
protected internal unsafe object MemberwiseClone()
{
// The remaining code is not shown
```

SHALLOW COPY VS. DEEP COPY

If you wonder about the terms shallow and deep, let me tell you that these are different types of cloning techniques. For now, you simply need to know that in the case of a shallow copy, simple type fields of a class are copied to the cloned instance, but for reference type fields, only the references are copied. So, in the case of a shallow copy, both the original and cloned instances point to the same reference. This may cause problems because an update on one object reflects the changes in the other object as well. To overcome this, you may need to employ the deep copy. In the Q&A session, you'll see a detailed discussion on the shallow copy and deep copy. If interested, you can also read the online link Object.MemberwiseClone Method (System) | Microsoft Learn that shows you the difference with examples.

Implementation

In Chapters 1 and 3, I constructed different types of cars using the Factory Method and Builder patterns. The Prototype pattern is often compared with those patterns. So, let us make cars one more time using this pattern (it helps you understand how different patterns can be used to produce similar products as well). However, before you see the implementation, I want you to read the following considerations to avoid any future confusion.

The Prototype design pattern can be implemented differently. Typically, you'll see an abstract class (or interface) that plays the role of an abstract prototype. This abstract prototype contains a cloning method that must be implemented by the concrete prototype(s). Then a client asks for a prototype and makes some changes in the prototype to make the desired object. I'm about to discuss different aspects of the upcoming implementation. **To make the code size short and simple, instead of making multiple concrete prototypes, I'll consider only one concrete prototype (Ford.cs) which inherits from an abstract prototype (Car.cs).** Once you understand the implementation, you should not have any problem to add more concrete prototypes. Here is a simple class diagram (see Figure 4-1) for your reference.

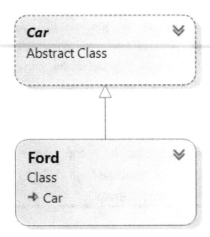

Figure 4-1. The Ford class (concrete prototype) inherits from the abstract class Car (abstract prototype)

Let's assume when a customer wants to purchase a car, he'd like to know about the following:

- The company that manufactured the car

- The model's name along with the color

- The price of the car (let us assume that it is the on-
  road price)

Now see the Car class that contains the most important method, called
CloneCar:

```
abstract class Car
{
    protected string company;
    protected Model model;
    public double price;
    public Car()
    {
        company = "Not set";
        model = new Model();
        price = 0;
    }
    public abstract void UpdateCar(string modelName, string
        color, double increasedPrice = 0);
    public abstract Car CloneCar();
}
```

I'd also like to draw your attention to the model field and the UpdateCar
method here. At first look, they may seem to be irreverent to you, and you
may ask:

- Why is the model a user-defined type?

- Why did I use an extra method – UpdateCar?

Let's see the explanations. Since the model is a user-defined type, the
shallow copy will not be sufficient in this implementation. **So, I provided
a deep copy implementation** (in fact, I chose this example to show you
the difference between a shallow copy and a deep copy). The updateCar
method will be used to analyze the effect of the copying technique.

Here is the Model class (using the primary constructor to make you familiar with it):

```
class Model(string modelName = "Not defined", string color = "
  Not set")
{
    public string modelName = modelName;
    public string color = color;
    public override string ToString()
    {
        return $"{modelName}, Color: {color}";
    }
}
```

The Ford class inherits from the car class and overrides the required methods. **By default, I create a Maverick Ford car and set the initial price to $30000. However, once I clone an existing Ford car, I'll reset the model to "not set" and set the default price to $25000.**

As said before, I am about to show you a deep copy implementation. You may note that a deep copy can be implemented in different ways. While implementing this mechanism in my demonstration, I followed the same approach that Microsoft used in the previous link. Let's see the complete Ford class now and seek help from the supportive comments (if needed):

```
class Ford : Car
{
    public Ford()
    {
        // Setting a default Ford car
        company = "Ford";
        model = new Model("Maverick", "Silver");
        price = 30000;
    }
```

```
public override void UpdateCar(string modelName, string
  color, double increasedPrice = 0)
{
    model.modelName = modelName;
    model.color = color;
    price += increasedPrice;
}
#region Applying the deep copy mechanism
public override Car CloneCar()
{
    // First making a shallow copy
    Ford fordClone = (Ford)MemberwiseClone();
    // Resetting the model info (this step is essential
    // for the deep copy)
    fordClone.model = new Model();
    // Setting a base price for the Ford car as well
    fordClone.price = 25000;
    return fordClone;
}
#endregion
public override string ToString()
{
    return $"Company: {company}, Model: {model}, Price:
      ${price} \n";
}
}
```

To understand the Prototype pattern, this concrete prototype will be enough. However, if you wish, you can also add more concrete prototypes.

Now you are ready to see the client code. Inside the client code, you'll see the following parts:

- First, I created a Ford class instance. Then, I created another instance by cloning the previous instance.

- After that, I made some changes in the cloned copy and displayed the details. **A change in the cloned copy should not be reflected in the original copy (and vice versa).** So, I verified the same here.

- Finally, I tested the reverse scenario where I made some changes in the initial car (from which the cloned car was built) and confirmed that these changes did not reflect in the cloned car.

To make things easy, let us visualize all the participants in the class diagram (Figure 4-2) (I also showed the Model class, so that you can see its fields and methods).

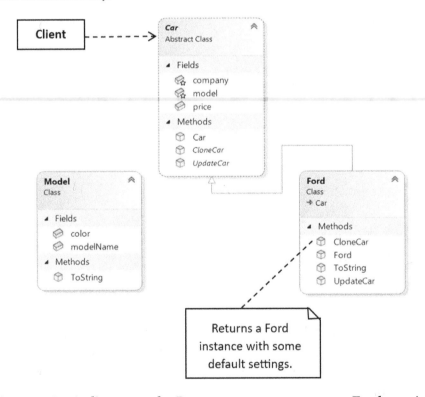

Figure 4-2. *A client uses the Prototype pattern to create Ford cars in Demonstration 1*

Demonstration 1

Here is the client code:

```
using static System.Console;

WriteLine("***Prototype Pattern Demo***\n");
// Getting a default Ford car
Car initialCar = new Ford();
WriteLine("The initial car details:");
WriteLine(initialCar);
WriteLine("Increasing the price by 2000 and displaying its
    details:");
initialCar.price += 2000;
WriteLine(initialCar);

WriteLine("Getting another Ford car with some default settings
    by cloning.");
Car clonedCar =(Ford) initialCar.CloneCar();
WriteLine("The cloned car details:");
WriteLine(clonedCar);
WriteLine("============================");

#region Discussing the advantage of deep copy
WriteLine("Changing the model, color, and price of the
    cloned car.");
clonedCar.UpdateCar("Ranger", "Blue", 10000);
WriteLine("Here are the cloned car details:");
WriteLine(clonedCar);
WriteLine("Verifying the initial car details as well.");
WriteLine(initialCar);
#endregion

WriteLine("============================");
```

```
WriteLine("Changing the model, color, and price of the initial
  car now.");
initialCar.UpdateCar("F-150", "Red", 20000);
WriteLine("After these changes, the initial car details:");
WriteLine(initialCar);
WriteLine("Verifying the cloned car details as well.");
WriteLine(clonedCar);
```

Output

Here is the output:

```
***Prototype Pattern Demo***

The initial car details:
Company: Ford, Model: Maverick, Color: Silver, Price: $30000

Increasing the price by 2000 and displaying its details:
Company: Ford, Model: Maverick, Color: Silver, Price: $32000

Getting another Ford car with some default settings by cloning.
The cloned car details:
Company: Ford, Model: Not defined, Color:  Not set,
Price: $25000

=============================
Changing the model, color, and price of the cloned car.
Here are the cloned car details:
Company: Ford, Model: Ranger, Color: Blue, Price: $35000

Verifying the initial car details as well.
Company: Ford, Model: Maverick, Color: Silver, Price: $32000

=============================
Changing the model, color, and price of the initial car now.
```

```
After these changes, the initial car details:
Company: Ford, Model: F-150, Color: Red, Price: $52000

Verifying the cloned car details as well.
Company: Ford, Model: Ranger, Color: Blue, Price: $35000
```

Analysis

You can see that initially I created a Maverick Ford car and set its price at $30000. Then I made a cloned instance from it. However, while cloning, I ensured that the model was not defined and the color was not set. Also, this cloned car's price was $25000.

Then I set the cloned car's model to **Ranger** and its color to **blue** and increased its price by $10000. **However, these changes did not impact the initial Maverick car.**

Finally, I incorporated some changes in the Maverick car (changed the model to **F-150** and its color to **red** and increased the price to $52000). **These changes did not impact the cloned car as well.**

These steps confirm that our Prototype pattern implementation worked as expected.

Q&A Session

Q4.1 "However, while cloning, I ensured that the model was not defined and the color was not set." Was there any specific thought behind this?
You could avoid these reset operations if you always create a Maverick car from a Maverick car (i.e., a cloned car has the same model as the original car). However, I wanted to create different models by cloning an existing car. This is why you saw those reset operations.

Author's note: In many implementations, you may see a dedicated method to perform the reset operation(s). However, my CloneCar method was not very big; so, I did not need to create such a method.

Q4.2 Does the Prototype pattern force me to prefer a deep copy over a shallow copy?

The classical GoF book says that a shallow copy is often sufficient. So, MemberwiseClone() in C# implementations can usually serve your needs. However, the classical GoF also says the following:

> ... cloning prototypes with complex structures usually requires a deep copy, because the clone and the original must be independent. Therefore you must ensure that the clone's components are clones of the prototype's components. Cloning forces you to decide what if anything will be shared.

Q4.3 The deep copy is expensive compared to the shallow copy. Isn't it?

True. However, while copying an object, there is no escape if you need to take care of all the references. Though a shallow copy is faster and less expensive, it serves your need if the original object has the primitive fields only. On the contrary, though a deep copy is expensive and slow, it is useful if the original object contains many fields that have references to other objects.

Q4.4 Can you show me a program that elaborates on the difference between a shallow copy and a deep copy in C#?

Let's comment out the code that is not required for the shallow copy in the CloneCar method of the Ford class as follows:

```
public override Car CloneCar()
{
    // First, making a shallow copy
    Ford fordClone = (Ford)MemberwiseClone();
    //// Resetting the model info ( this step is essential
    //// for the deep copy)]
    //fordClone.model = new Model();
    //// Setting a base price for the Ford car as well
    //fordClone.price = 25000;
    return fordClone;
}
```

Now if you execute the program again, you'll see that **the edits in the cloned car changed the original car as well (and vice versa).** I have highlighted the key changes in bold. Here is the sample output:

```
***Prototype Pattern Demo***

The initial car details:
Company: Ford, Model: Maverick, Color: Silver, Price: $30000

Increasing the price by 2000 and displaying its details:
Company: Ford, Model: Maverick, Color: Silver, Price: $32000

Getting another Ford car with some default settings by cloning.
The cloned car details:
Company: Ford, Model: Maverick, Color: Silver, Price: $32000
==============================
Changing the model, color, and price of the cloned car.
Here are the cloned car details:
Company: Ford, Model: Ranger, Color: Blue, Price: $42000

Verifying the initial car details as well.
Company: Ford, Model: Ranger, Color: Blue, Price: $32000

==============================
Changing the model, color, and price of the initial car now.
After these changes, the initial car details:
Company: Ford, Model: F-150, Color: Red, Price: $52000

Verifying the cloned car details as well.
Company: Ford, Model: F-150, Color: Red, Price: $42000
```

Why did this happen? The MemberwiseClone method created a shallow copy by creating a new object, and then it copied the non-static fields from the original object to the new object. If there exists a value type field in the original object, a bit-by-bit copy is performed. But if the field is a reference type, this method will copy the reference, not the actual object.

Let's try to understand the mechanism with a simple diagram (see Figure 4-3). Suppose you have an object X1, and it has a reference to another object, Y1.

Figure 4-3. *X1 has a reference to Y1*

After a shallow copy of X1, a new object (say, X2) will be created that will also reference Y1 (see Figure 4-4).

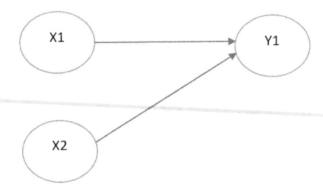

Figure 4-4. *After a shallow copy of X1, the new object X2 also references Y1*

On the contrary, after a deep copy of X1, a new object (say, X3) will be created, and X3 will have a reference to the new object Y3 which is a copy of Y1 (see Figure 4-5).

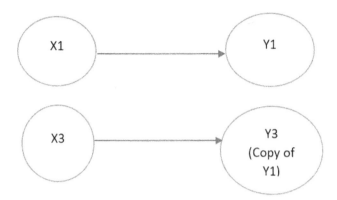

Figure 4-5. *After a deep copy of X1, the new object X3 references Y3 which is a copy of Y1*

Q4.5 "A deep copy can be implemented in different ways." Can you please elaborate?

I'd like to follow the official guidelines from Object.MemberwiseClone Method (System) | Microsoft Learn that suggest four different approaches. Interestingly, you saw one of them already in Demonstration 1. How? Let me draw your attention again to the following method:

```
public override Car CloneCar()
{
    // First, making a shallow copy
    Ford fordClone = (Ford)MemberwiseClone();
    // Resetting the model info ( this step is essential for
    the deep copy)]
    fordClone.model = new Model();
    // Setting a base price for the Ford car as well
    fordClone.price = 25000;
    return fordClone;
}
```

Notice that I called the MemberwiseClone method to create a shallow copy first and then assigned a new object to the model field that is nothing but a Model instance.

For a deep copy, the previous link also suggests some additional approaches. I summarized them as follows:

- Use a copy constructor.

- Apply a serializing mechanism.

- Use reflection with recursion.

Q4.6 What are the advantages of using the Prototype design pattern?
Here are some important usages:

- You do not want to modify the existing object and experiment on that.

- You can include or discard products at runtime.

- To incorporate a minor change, you can avoid creating a new object from scratch.

- You can focus on the key activities rather than focusing on complicated instance creation processes. For example, once you ignore the complex object creation processes, you can simply start with cloning or coping objects and implementing the remaining parts.

- You want to examine the upcoming behavior of the new object before you fully implement it.

Q4.7 What are the challenges associated with using the Prototype design pattern?
Here are some challenges:

- Each subclass needs to implement the cloning or copying mechanism. However, there are situations where a particular subclass may not want to support cloning.

- Implementing the cloning mechanism is also challenging if there are circular references.

Q4.8 Should we register different prototypes in a single class?

Good question. In my example, I created the first instance inside the client code. However, you can always hide the instantiation from clients. Using a common class that holds all the prototypes can solve this problem. In fact, the classical GoF book also promotes this idea by saying:

> *When the number of prototypes in a system isn't fixed (that is, they can be created and destroyed dynamically), keep a registry of available prototypes. Clients won't manage prototypes themselves but will store and retrieve them from the registry. A client will ask the registry for a prototype before cloning it.*

Q4.9 How does the Prototype pattern differ from the Factory Method pattern?

The Factory Method promotes subclassing. In Chapter 1, you saw different factories produce different vehicles. For example, SportsFactory produced sports cars and sports motorcycles, whereas the TraditionalFactory produced traditional cars and traditional motorcycles. These were specialized factories that formed a hierarchy of creator classes. On the contrary, the Prototype pattern focuses on cloning to make a new object. So, this pattern does not force you to form a creator class hierarchy.

Let's move on to the final chapter and continue learning another interesting pattern called Dependency Injection.

CHAPTER 5

Dependency Injection Pattern

Dependency Injection is a useful design pattern. Microsoft (see Dependency injection - .NET | Microsoft Learn) states:

> .NET supports the dependency injection (DI) software design pattern, which is a technique for achieving Inversion of Control (IoC) between classes and their dependencies.

This chapter discusses this pattern using simple examples.

Concept

The importance of this pattern will become clear once you understand the need. So, let me show you a program that can produce an expected result, but is challenging to maintain.

A Sample Program

Throughout the book, we made lots of cars. Let us work with them one more time. This time, the Car is a simple class:

```
class Car
{
```

© Vaskaran Sarcar 2025
V. Sarcar, *Creational Design Patterns in C#*, Apress Pocket Guides,
https://doi.org/10.1007/979-8-8688-1567-6_5

```
    public string Run(int speed)
    {
        return $"{this} at {speed} mph";
    }
    public override string ToString()
    {
        return "car";
    }
}
```

Let's create another class (Driver) that'd like to drive the cars (i.e., the Car instances):

```
using static System.Console;
class Driver
{
    private readonly Car _car;
    public Driver()
    {
        _car = new Car();
    }
    public void Drive(int speed)
    {
        WriteLine($"The driver can drive a {_car.Run(speed)}");
    }
}
```

To make things easy, before you see the client code, let us visualize the class diagram (Figure 5-1).

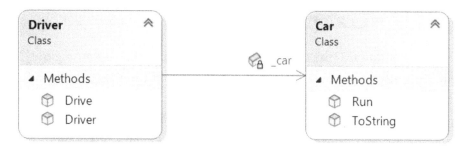

Figure 5-1. *The Driver class depends on the Car class*

Demonstration 1

Let me show you a sample client code:

// DI_Demo1_Client.cs

```
Driver driver = new();
driver.Drive(100);
```

Output

There is no surprise that when you execute this program, you'll see the following output:

```
The driver can drive a car at 100 mph
```

Introducing Dependency Injection

In the previous program, the Driver class created a Car instance inside its constructor. **It's like you book a car and the driver brings a car for you. In this case, the driver depends on the car while traveling and gets a payment from you.** However, real-life situations can be more demanding. Let's look at some real-world scenarios as follows.

Real-Life Example

In Demonstration 1, the driver depends on the car. So, maintaining the car is his responsibility. However, it is possible that you may not like the driver's car. Instead, you'd like to travel with your car and hire a driver (let's assume that you do not want to drive). In this case, the driver can fully focus on his job (i.e., driving), and his payment is no longer dependent on the car. In this case, the driver does not worry about the car's maintenance. This example shows that the driver's dependency on the car is reduced.

POINT TO NOTE

In Demonstration 1, a `Car` object was created inside the `Driver` class's constructor. This code segment reflects that the `Driver` class was coupled with the `Car` class. DI primarily targets to loose the coupling between classes to make them easily reusable, testable, and maintainable. As a result, the concurrent development becomes easy as well.

I also want you to note that the `Car` class can have additional dependencies as well. To make the discussion easy, I made this class truly simple.

Finding other real-life examples is easy as well. For example, when I worked for my employer, I did not need to worry about the servicing of the laptop. However, for my personal laptop, I may need to go to a laptop service shop if it starts malfunctioning or requires any improvements. You can see that my dependency on a laptop varies according to the situation.

Computer World Example

The official link `https://learn.microsoft.com/en-us/dotnet/core/extensions/dependency-injection` states the following:

> *Dependency injection in .NET is a built-in part of the framework, along with configuration, logging, and the options pattern.*

So, there is no wonder that .NET, especially with ASP.NET Core, has built-in DI support. You may note that the Java Spring Framework also supports the concept.

POINT TO NOTE

This chapter gives you the core idea of DI. You can implement these ideas in a different programming language (such as Java) as well. I recommend that after finishing this chapter, you also read about ".NET dependency injection" from the online link `https://learn.microsoft.com/en-us/dotnet/core/extensions/dependency-injection`.

Types of DI

While applying DI, you'd like to avoid the situation where a class creates its own dependencies. Instead, you'd like to use an external entity (often termed an injector) that will provide those dependencies. This is why while improving Demonstration 1, you'd not allow the `Driver` class to create its own dependencies (`Car` class in our example).

Now the question is how to implement the idea? You can implement it in various ways, such as

- Constructor injection

- Setter injection (often called property injection)

- Method injection

- Interface injection

Let's start the discussion with the constructor injection (CI).

Constructor Injection

In this section, you'll see two programs. In the first program, I'll show you a simple technique to overcome the tight coupling between the Driver class and the Car class. In the next program, I'll enhance the capability of the program.

Demonstration 2

See the new look of the Driver class:

```
using static System.Console;
class Driver
{
    private readonly Car _car;
    public Driver(Car car)
    {
        _car = car; // Injecting the car
    }
    public void Drive(int speed)
    {
        WriteLine($"The driver can drive a {_car.Run(speed)}");
    }
}
```

Using the primary constructor, you can further make it concise as follows:

```
using static System.Console;

class Driver(Car car)
{
    private readonly Car _car = car;
    public void Drive(int speed)
    {
```

```
      WriteLine($"The driver can drive a {_car.Run(speed)}");
   }
}
```

Now the `Driver` constructor does not create the `Car` instance. Instead, a client of this class will be responsible for supplying the `Car` instance. As a result, the `Driver` class is no longer dependent on the `Car` class. Here is a sample client code:

// DI_Demo2_Client.cs

```
Car car = new();
Driver driver = new(car);
driver.Drive(100);
```

Output

Upon executing this program, you'll see the same output:

```
The driver can drive a car at 100 mph
```

Enhancing the Program

Let's assume that the driver is a smart guy who can also drive a different type of vehicle, such as a bus. How can you accommodate his capability in this program? You guessed it right! You can introduce an interface and inherit the concrete classes from it.

POINT TO NOTE

Since I'll reuse this vehicle hierarchy in the upcoming examples as well, I created a class library project (I named it `VehicleLibraryForDI`) and placed these constructs there. For the same reason, I needed to enhance the corresponding visibilities (I made them `public`).

Here is the interface, called IVehicle:

```
public interface IVehicle
{
    string Run(int speed);
}
```

Now the Car class can inherit from it:

```
public class Car : IVehicle
{
    public string Run(int speed)
    {
        return $"{this} at {speed} mph";
    }
    public override string ToString()
    {
        return "car";
    }
}
```

The Bus class is very similar to the Car class. Let's see it now:

```
public class Bus : IVehicle
{
    public string Run(int speed)
    {
        return $"{this} at {speed} mph";
    }
    public override string ToString()
    {
        return "bus";
    }
}
```

It's time to adjust the `Driver` class as well (notice the key changes in bold):

```
using static System.Console;
class Driver(IVehicle vehicle)
{
    private readonly IVehicle _vehicle = vehicle;
    public void Drive(int speed)
    {
        WriteLine($"The driver can drive a {_vehicle.Run
        (speed)}");
    }
}
```

To make things easy, before you see the client code, let us visualize all the participants in the class diagram (Figure 5-2).

Figure 5-2. *The Driver class now knows about the IVehicle type, but not a concrete implementation (such as Car or Bus) of it*

Demonstration 3

Now, see the client code:

// DI_Demo3_Client.cs

```
IVehicle vehicle = new Car();
Driver driver = new(vehicle);
driver.Drive(100);

vehicle = new Bus();
driver = new(vehicle);
driver.Drive(150);
```

Output

Once you execute this program, you'll see the following output:

```
The driver can drive a car at 100 mph
The driver can drive a bus at 150 mph
```

Q&A Session

Q5.1 Does the constructor injection force me to use an interface instead of a concrete class?

No. However, in Demonstration 3, I used multiple vehicle types. This was the primary reason for using the interface IVehicle.

In addition, one of the key design principles in OOP is to program to an interface, but not an implementation. So, it's a good practice to avoid using the concrete types.

POINT TO NOTE

Developers often use the phrase "you need to implement the interface." It
does not always mean that you need to implement a C# interface. It is often
used as a generic term where they intend to say that a concrete class needs to
implement an abstract class or an interface (i.e., a supertype from which the
concrete class is derived).

However, these do not force you to consider constructor injection
using an interface type. Demonstration 2 showed you an example without
using an interface.

Setter Injection

You can also have setter injection (often called property injection). To
demonstrate this, instead of making an IVehicle field, let's make it a
property. Here is the new look of the Driver class (notice that this time,
you do not need to define any constructor):

```
using static System.Console;

class Driver
{
    // Using an auto property and making it required
    public required IVehicle Vehicle { get; set; }
    public void Drive(int speed)
    {
        WriteLine($"The driver can drive a {Vehicle.Run
        (speed)}");
    }
}
```

You do not need to make any other change for the following demonstration. To confirm this, let me show you the class diagram as well (see Figure 5-3).

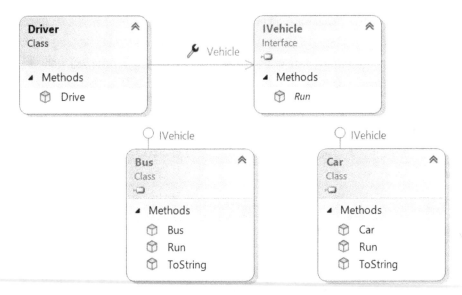

Figure 5-3. *The Driver class has the Vehicle property that can be set in the client code*

Demonstration 4

Let's see how a client can handle the change now:

```
// DI_Demo4_Client.cs

IVehicle vehicle = new Car();
Driver driver = new()
{
    Vehicle = vehicle
};
driver.Drive(100);
```

```
// Creating a new vehicle
vehicle = new Bus();
// Letting the driver drive the new vehicle( i.e. a bus)
driver.Vehicle = vehicle;
driver.Drive(150);
```

Output

There is no surprise that you'll get the following output:

```
The driver can drive a car at 100 mph
The driver can drive a bus at 150 mph
```

Analysis

Notice the client code again. This time, you can allow the driver to drive a new vehicle (bus) without creating a new instance of the Driver class. However, in the case of constructor dependency, this flexibility was absent.

Q&A Session

Q5.2 Why did you make the Vehicle property required?
I wanted to make sure that this property is set before you invoke the Drive method. You must acknowledge that if this property is null, invoking the Drive method on a Driver instance can cause an unwanted outcome. In that case, you need to introduce a null check before you exercise the line WriteLine($"The driver can drive a {Vehicle.Run(speed)}");.

Q5.3 Nowadays, doing a null check is easy. For example, by writing the line WriteLine($"The driver can drive a {Vehicle?.Run(speed)}"); **in the** Drive **method, I can easily avoid the unwanted situations. Isn't it?**
You can avoid the NullReferenceException, but you will see an unwanted output. For example, the following segment in the client code

```
Driver driver = new()
```

```
{
    //Vehicle = vehicle
    Vehicle = null // testing for null scenario
};
driver.Drive(100);
```

will produce the following output:

```
The driver can drive a
```

You can see that this is an incomplete line that does not make any sense.

Q5.4 Can we combine different injection techniques?
Yes, you can. For example, while creating a `Driver` instance, I could inject a vehicle using constructor injection (following Demonstration 3). Later, I could set a new vehicle for the same `Driver` instance (following Demonstration 4).

Method Injection

The CI allows you to pass dependencies as arguments to the constructors. You can do the same to a specific method as well. Let me show you an example by updating the previous program. Here is the new look of the `Driver` class:

```
using static System.Console;

class Driver
{
    public void Drive(IVehicle vehicle,int speed)
    {
```

```
    WriteLine($"The driver can drive a {vehicle.Run
    (speed)}");
  }
}
```

You do not need any other change for the following demonstration.

Demonstration 5

Let's see how a client can handle the change:

// DI_Demo5_Client.cs

```
IVehicle vehicle = new Car();
Driver driver = new();
driver.Drive(vehicle,100);

// Creating a new vehicle
vehicle = new Bus();
// Letting the driver drive the new vehicle( i.e. a bus)
driver.Drive(vehicle, 150);
```

Output

Once again, you'll see the following output:

```
The driver can drive a car at 100 mph
The driver can drive a bus at 150 mph
```

Analysis

Once again, the same driver could drive both a car and a bus.

Q&A Session

Q5.5 When should I prefer method injections?

Method injections are useful for injecting temporary dependencies. They can also serve you when you have different implementations for various method calls.

Interface Injection

This time, I'll discuss the interface injection technique. Its overall architecture is a little bit complex compared to the previous DI techniques. However, in the long run, you can enjoy the benefits.

Until now, drivers have used the vehicles. However, there are other categories of people who can use these vehicles. For example, if a car does not provide a satisfactory service, a driver can take it to a service center where a mechanic can fix the issue. In this scenario, the driver and the mechanic both work on the same car.

How can you update your program to accommodate this scenario? You got it right! You can use an interface from which the corresponding classes (for drivers and mechanics) will inherit. So, let us start with the following interface:

```
interface IVehicleUser
{
    void SetVehicle (IVehicle vehicle);
    void Drive(int speed);
}
```

Now, the Driver class can implement the interface as follows:

```
using static System.Console;
class Driver : IVehicleUser
{
```

```
private  IVehicle _vehicle;
 public void SetVehicle(IVehicle vehicle)
 {
    _vehicle = vehicle;
 }
 public void Drive(int speed)
 {
     WriteLine($"The driver can drive a {_vehicle.Run
     (speed)}");
 }
}
```

We do not need any other change for the following demonstration. Let me show you the class diagram as well (see Figure 5-4).

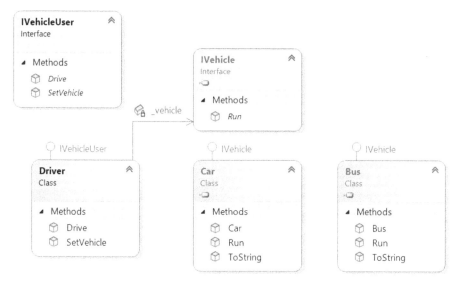

Figure 5-4. *The class diagram after the interface injection*

Demonstration 6

Let's see how a client can handle these changes:

```
// DI_Demo6_Client.cs
IVehicle vehicle = new Car();
IVehicleUser driver = new Driver();
driver.SetVehicle(vehicle);
// Let the driver drive a car
driver.Drive(100);

// Creating a new vehicle
vehicle = new Bus();
// Letting the driver drive the new vehicle( i.e. a bus)
driver.Drive(150);
```

Output

There is no surprise that you'll get the following output:

```
The driver can drive a car at 100 mph
The driver can drive a bus at 150 mph
```

Q&A Session

**Q5.6 In Demonstration 6, the Driver class implements the IVehicleUser
interface that sets the dependency. In other words, the dependency is
injected through an interface method. I understand that it allows the
Driver class to get the dependency from an external source. However,
at the end, I can see that the same driver could drive both a car and
a bus in this demonstration as well. Then why did you complicate
the thing?**

This design gives you more flexibility. Only professional drivers don't need to be the drivers; a novice learner or a mechanic can also use a vehicle. You may argue by saying that anyone who is sitting in the driver's seat is a driver. If you think like this, let me tell you that instead of making the `Driver` class, I could make classes such as `ProfessionalDriver`, `NoviceDriver`, or `Mechanic` that implement the `IVehicleUser` interface. Now, you see three different kinds of vehicle users who need the required services (for transportation, testing, or repairing) from the external source(s).

Q5.7 Can you summarize the differences between the different Dependency Injection techniques?
In the case of constructor injections, **you provide all the dependencies at the time of instantiation. You cannot change these dependencies after the instantiation process**.

In the case of setter DI or method DI, **you can alter the dependencies after the object is created**. For example, in the corresponding demonstrations (Demonstration 4 and Demonstration 5), you saw the instantiation of the `Driver` class only once. Still, you have seen that the same driver was able to drive both a car and a bus. However, you need to be careful. It is because **if the dependencies are not set properly, you'll encounter unwanted outcomes. On the contrary, the constructor injection ensures that a target class cannot be instantiated without the necessary dependencies**.

The interface DI is **comparatively complex compared to others. However, it provides more flexibility** that has already been discussed in the previous Q&A (5.6).

You can see that each approach has its own pros and cons. So, choose the approach that can make your application better. As said before, if needed, you can combine multiple approaches as well.

Q5.8 I often hear the term Dependency Inversion. How does it differ from Dependency Injection?

Dependency Injection (DI) is a design pattern/technique that you learned in this chapter. Dependency Inversion is a design principle (often termed DIP) that promotes loose coupling and abstraction. *DIP can be achieved through DI.*

I have discussed DIP in detail in my other book *Simple and Efficient Programming with C#, Second Edition* (Apress, 2022). For now, let me pick some portions from that book to give you a basic idea.

DIP tells two important things:

- A high-level concrete class should not depend on a low-level concrete class. Instead, both should depend on abstractions.

- Abstractions should not depend upon details. Instead, the details should depend upon abstractions.

POINT TO NOTE

In his book *Agile Principles, Patterns, and Practices in C#*, Robert C. Martin explains that a traditional software development model in earlier days tended to create software where high-level modules used to depend on low-level modules. But in OOP, a well-designed program opposes the idea. It inverts the dependency structure that often results from a traditional procedural method. This is the reason he used the word "Inversion" in this principle.

Now compare the figures – Figure 5-1 and Figure 5-2 – again. In Figure 5-1, the Driver class (the high-level concrete class) depended on the Car class (the low-level concrete class). However, after the constructor injection, in Figure 5-2, the Driver class and the Car class both were dependent on IVehicle. This structure fulfills the criteria for the

DIP. How? Notice that this time, the `Driver` class targets the abstraction `IVehicle`, instead of a concrete implementation (`Car`). This gave you the flexibility to consider a new vehicle type (`Bus`) without altering the existing classes.

If you dive deep into the DIP, you'll understand the essence of the second part of the DIP as well. It is important because if an interface needs to change to support one of its clients, other clients can be impacted due to the change. This is why you should consider designing `IVehicle` to fulfill the need of the `Driver` class only (for our example).

So, you can see that **DIP can be achieved through DI**. However, while working on DI, you'll often hear that it is used to achieve **Inversion of Control (IoC)**, which is a broader principle. Using the concept of IoC, you can pass the control of object creation and management from your application to an external framework or container. **A detailed discussion on IoC and DIP is beyond the scope of this book.**

POINT TO NOTE

Manually implementing Dependency Injections across a large code base is a challenging task. In that case, you can take help from a framework that supports this concept. For example, apart from the built-in supports, you can use **Autofac** (an IoC container for Microsoft .NET) to express dependencies in your C# project. Need other examples? Let's see the developers' thoughts at https://stackoverflow.com/questions/21288/which-net-dependency-injection-frameworks-are-worth-looking-into.

Q5.9 Do you consider DI as a creational design pattern?

At first look, DI may not appear as a creational pattern as per the definition of the classic GoF book. Still, it is often associated with creational patterns because it can influence how you create (and manage) objects in a system. In fact, if you see the interview with Erich Gamma, Richard Helm, and

Ralph Johnson – Design Patterns 15 Years Later: An Interview with Erich Gamma, Richard Helm, and Ralph Johnson I InformIT or Ralph Johnson's talk at JDD2015 - Twenty-one Years of Design Patterns (Ralph Johnson) - YouTube – you will see that DI is considered as a creational design pattern.

However, at the beginning of this chapter, you saw that Microsoft (see Dependency injection - .NET I Microsoft Learn) considers DI as a technique for achieving Inversion of Control (IoC). Since IoC is an architectural pattern (see Design Patterns - Wikipedia), you can say that DI falls under the broader category of Architectural patterns.

Interestingly, Wikipedia (see the same link) tagged Dependency Injection and Method Chaining in "Other Patterns." I already used method chaining while implementing the Builder pattern (see Demonstration 2 of Chapter 3). In the same way, you can use DI with other patterns to make a nice application. So, according to me, understanding the pattern is more important than tagging it with a category. If you still force me to pick only one general category for DI, I'd like to tag it as an Architectural pattern.

Congratulations! You have completed all the patterns in this book. You can now implement these ideas in various projects. I believe that you will find these patterns helpful even if you use a different programming language. I hope that you'll value the effort.

Happy coding!

APPENDIX A

What's Next?

This book covered five useful creational design patterns with many examples. After completing this book, I hope you have a fair idea about those patterns. Now, you read the related topics from other books, articles, or blogs. However, do not forget to read the classic GoF book (listed below). Though it was published long ago, you'll find this book helpful in 2025 as well. This is why it is still a bestseller on Amazon!

The next step is to exercise these patterns in your programs, keep experimenting with new code, and learn more. We all know that practice makes a man perfect.

You may note that I also keep experimenting with patterns and have written several books on design patterns using C# and Java. For example, *Java Design Patterns*, Third Edition (Apress, 2022), and *Design Patterns in C#*, Second Edition (Apress, 2020), covered all 23 GoF patterns and some additional patterns. They also discussed anti-patterns and commonly asked questions on design patterns. One of my recent books, *Parallel Programming with C# and .NET*, discussed the Task-based Asynchronous Pattern (TAP) and related topics. If interested, you can learn those patterns from these books.

In the following list, you will also see a few more books from which I got many new insights. **Though not all of them are C# and .NET specific**, I believe that they can be equally effective for you. You can learn more from these books (or their updated editions).

© Vaskaran Sarcar 2025
V. Sarcar, *Creational Design Patterns in C#*, Apress Pocket Guides,
https://doi.org/10.1007/979-8-8688-1567-6

Books

Here is my recommended list of books for you:

- *Design Patterns: Elements of Reusable Object-Oriented Software* by Erich Gamma et al. (Addison-Wesley, 1995)

- *Java Design Patterns* by Vaskaran Sarcar, Third Edition (Apress, 2022)

- *Head First Design Patterns* by Eric Freeman and Elisabeth Robson, Second Edition (O'Reilly, 2021)

- *Design Patterns in C#*, Second Edition, by Vaskaran Sarcar (Apress, 2020)

- *C# Design Pattern Essentials* by Tony Bevis (Ability First Limited, 2012)

- *Design Patterns For Dummies* by Steve Holzner (Wiley Publishing, Inc, 2006)

Other Resources

In today's world, online platforms are very powerful. So, you can always learn from Google, Stack Overflow, Quora, YouTube, LinkedIn Learning, or Udemy. You can use these online platforms to learn not only design patterns but almost anything you want. However, you must validate the content.

Finally, in each chapter, I referred to some links in our discussions and Q&A Sessions. You can have a detailed look at those links to learn more.

APPENDIX B

Other Books by the Author

The following list includes other Apress books by the author:

- *Python Bootcamp* (Apress, 2025)

- *Task Programming in C# and .NET* (Apress, 2025)

- *Parallel Programming with C# and .NET* (Apress, 2024)

- *Introducing Functional Programming Using C#* (Apress, 2023)

- *Simple and Efficient Programming in C#*, Second Edition (Apress, 2022)

- *Test Your Skills in C# Programming* (Apress, 2022)

- *Java Design Patterns*, Third Edition (Apress, 2022)

- *Simple and Efficient Programming in C#* (Apress, 2021)

- *Design Patterns in C#*, Second Edition (Apress, 2020)

- *Getting Started with Advanced C#* (Apress, 2020)

- *Interactive Object-Oriented Programming in Java*, Second Edition (Apress, 2019)

- *Java Design Patterns*, Second Edition (Apress, 2019)

© Vaskaran Sarcar 2025
V. Sarcar, *Creational Design Patterns in C#*, Apress Pocket Guides,
https://doi.org/10.1007/979-8-8688-1567-6

- *Design Patterns in C#* (Apress, 2018)

- *Interactive C#* (Apress, 2017)

- *Interactive Object-Oriented Programming in Java* (Apress, 2016)

- *Java Design Patterns* (Apress, 2016)

The following list includes his non-Apress books:

- *Python Bookcamp* (Amazon, 2021)

- *Operating System: Computer Science Interview Series* (Createspace, 2014)

To learn more about these books, you can refer to any of the following links:

- `https://amazon.com/author/vaskaran_sarcar`

- `https://link.springer.com/search?newsearch=true &query=vaskaran+sarcar&content-type=book&dateFr om=&dateTo=&sortBy=newestFirst`

GPSR Compliance
The European Union's (EU) General Product Safety Regulation (GPSR) is a set
of rules that requires consumer products to be safe and our obligations to
ensure this.

If you have any concerns about our products, you can contact us on

ProductSafety@springernature.com

In case Publisher is established outside the EU, the EU authorized
representative is:

Springer Nature Customer Service Center GmbH
Europaplatz 3
69115 Heidelberg, Germany

www.ingramcontent.com/pod-product-compliance
Lightning Source LLC
LaVergne TN
LVHW051641050326
832903LV00022B/841

9 7 9 8 8 6 8 8 1 5 6 6 9